T·A·K·I·N·G
GLASNOST
SERIOUSLY

T·A·K·I·N·G

GLASNOST

SERIOUSLY

TOWARD AN OPEN SOVIET UNION

MICHAEL NOVAK

AMERICAN ENTERPRISE INSTITUTE FOR PUBLIC POLICY RESEARCH
Washington, D.C.

Michael Novak holds the George Frederick Jewett Chair in Religion, Philosophy, and Public Policy at the American Enterprise Institute, where he serves as director of Social and Political Studies. He was appointed head of the U.S. delegation to the Experts' Meeting on Human Contacts of the Conference on Security and Cooperation in Europe and served as a presidential adviser to the Ford and Carter administrations. Mr. Novak has published numerous books including *The Spirit of Democratic Capitalism, Moral Clarity in the Nuclear Age, Confession of a Catholic, Freedom with Justice: Catholic Social Thought and Liberal Institutions,* and *Will It Liberate? Questions about Liberation Theology.*

Distributed by arrangement with

UPA, Inc.
4720 Boston Way
Lanham, MD 20706
3 Henrietta Street
London WC2E 8LU England

Library of Congress Cataloging-in-Publication Data

Novak, Michael.
Taking Glasnost seriously.
1. Conference on Security and Cooperation in Europe
(1975 : Helsinki, Finland) 2. CSCE Experts Meeting on Human Contact
(1986 : Bern, Switzerland) 3. Soviet Union—Emigration and
immigration. 4. Civil rights—Soviet Union. I. Title.
JX1393.C65N68   1988   327.1'7'094   87–34895 CIP
ISBN 0-8447-3641-4
ISBN 0-8447-3642-2 (pbk.)

AEI Studies 465

Printed in the United States of America

Contents

Preface

The Bern Experts' Meeting, including its two weeks of preliminary meetings, lasted a total of forty working week days—although weekends, too, were often heavily scheduled with group trips or private meetings. A frank description of the hurried conditions under which the speeches collected below were composed would defy belief. The schedulers of international meetings allow frightfully little time for actual writing. The duties of an ambassador—to the thirty-four other ambassadors present, to the public, to the press, to his own staff, and to steady communication with his capital—fill every free minute of the day. From eight in the morning until eleven P.M. or midnight, there are duties to be met. In wanting to write my own speeches, I had to fight for minutes and struggle to complete even paragraphs.

The assistance of staff was, of course, tremendous. In our case, experts in various areas drew up "building blocks" for speeches, accumulated the factual data, verified details, and suggested arguments. They also criticized each of my full drafts as it emerged, pointing out flaws and potential misunderstandings. The U.S. team in Bern—staffed both by the State Department and by the Helsinki Commission of the U.S. Congress—was expert, extremely well prepared, and invariably generous with overtime and frantic work. I can never thank them enough: Ambassador Sol Polansky and Sam Wise of the Helsinki Commission, who provided experienced leadership throughout; Ambassador Max Kampelman, who came over from Geneva for one extremely important appearance at Bern; Julien LeBourgeois, the talented and classy officer assigned by the State Department to the Commission on Security and Cooperation in Europe; and many others from the State Department or the Helsinki Commission: Ed Alexander, Debby Burns, Bruce Connuck, Tom Countryman, Orest Deychakiwsky, Barbara Edwards, John Finerty, Dolores Fitch, Michael Hathaway, Carol Medeiros, Golde Rhodes, John Schmidt, Earlina Smith, John Spiegel, and Mildred Zyvoloski. A special word of thanks is due to two distinguished experts who each joined briefly and with spirit in our work: George Urban and William Korey.

Michael Novak

Introduction

Jeane J. Kirkpatrick

It is a pleasure to introduce the speeches of Michael Novak to the 1986 Helsinki Review Conference on Human Contacts. Novak's speeches are an eloquent reminder of the human meaning of the Helsinki Accords.

The most interesting accord negotiated between the Soviet Union and the West is the Helsinki Agreement on Cooperation and Security in Europe signed in 1975 by thirty-five countries including the United States and the USSR. The Helsinki Accords link security to respect for human rights and provide for regular meetings to review compliance of each country with the commitments made in signing the Helsinki Accords.

Alone among international agreements of recent years, the Helsinki Accords focus not only on relations among governments but also on relations between governments and their own citizens. "Basket Three" of the Helsinki Accords committed governments to promote broader contact between people, to promote mutual understanding and concord, to encourage human contacts across state boundaries and ideologies, to facilitate the reunification of families, to permit emigration with the right to return, to travel, and to respect the rights of minorities and minority cultures. The Helsinki Accords also affirmed the right of people to know their rights. The accords addressed real hardships and aimed—or purported to aim—at codifying for European civilization common understandings of the basic rights of citizens and obligations of governments. Taken at face value, the Helsinki Accords reflected agreed-upon standards of civilized conduct. In fact, no consensus on civilized behavior existed then or now. By the time the accords were signed, hundreds of thousands of Soviet Jews had been denied the right to leave the Soviet Union. Instead of permission to depart, their applications to leave led to interrogation, denial of work permits, or imprisonment on various pretexts. Such "refuseniks" eagerly awaited Soviet ratification of the Helsinki Accords, though they knew, as Anatoly Shcharansky wrote: "Every time the Soviet Union undertakes new international obligations, such as the Helsinki Accords, the authorities do their best to frighten all the people who can make use of them."

Nonetheless refuseniks, Estonians, Lithuanians, separated married couples, and others have sought to make use of the rights publicly affirmed and ratified by Leonid Brezhnev on September 18, 1975. Human rights activists in Czechoslovakia, Poland, and the "autonomous republics" of the Soviet Union (that are neither autonomous nor republics—the Ukraine, Lithuania, Georgia, Estonia, and Latvia) formed Public Groups to Promote Implementation of the Helsinki Agreement. For their trouble, many were arrested, imprisoned under harsh conditions. The treatment of Yuri Orlov, Anatoly Shcharansky, Elena Bonner, other Helsinki monitors, and others testifies not only to the denial of rights affirmed at Helsinki but also to the systematic persecution of those who sought to claim those solemnly affirmed rights.

Bitter at the continuing suppression of rights and the punishment of those who claimed them, a group of distinguished Soviet émigré intellectuals called on the West last year to abandon the agreement, "which has turned into a repressive tool in the hands of Soviet authorities . . . until the Soviets prove by concrete actions their readiness to observe these basic rights." They wrote:

> We have done our best to make the Helsinki Agreement serve peace and democracy. However, we can no longer associate ourselves with the agreement which not only failed to serve its humanitarian purposes, but even to protect its most sincere supporters, an agreement which has turned into a repressive tool in the hands of Soviet authorities. We appeal to the Western governments to make the Helsinki Agreement null and void.

Their frustration and disappointment are easy to understand. It is not clear how an agreement continuously violated by one of the parties can retain value or how a "compliance" process to which the Soviet Union is a party can avoid degenerating into an exercise in cynicism.

Michael Novak's speeches at the review conference on human contacts (Bern, Switzerland, 1986) demonstrate how and why the Helsinki Accords and the review process can reinforce the values affirmed in the Helsinki Accords—despite their systematic violation by some of the signatories. Novak's speeches illuminate, illustrate, and explore the human values embodied in the accords on human contacts. They explain how, by honoring the accords, governments enrich the lives of their citizens and how, in betraying these commitments, governments impoverish the lives of persons, families, societies, and nations.

Novak tells us that at the signing of the accords eleven years ago

Sir Alec Douglas-Home, then the British Foreign Secretary, observed, "If we do not improve the life of ordinary people at this conference, we shall be asked—and with justice—what all our fine words and diplomatic phrases have achieved." Novak makes this standard his own:

> Ordinary people are our theme. Our mandate is to improve their lives . . . to seek improvement in their contacts with other human beings and to discern the impediments, obstacles, and barbed wire walls, the tangles of law and administrative breakdowns, that interrupt such contacts.

In exploring and explaining the ways human contacts and obstacles to them affect the lives of persons and societies, Novak lays bare the human significance of governmental policies.

His discussion is characterized by clarity and concreteness. He eschews polemics and abstractions in favor of a steady focus on the human meaning of the accords' provisions concerning human contacts. His analysis is probing, his description lucid. He describes the pleas received by the delegation from relatives in the Baltic states, the Ukraine, and Russia, unable to visit family members from whom they have been long separated. He tells us of pleas of spouses, separated for years by refusal of visa requests. Eleven couples had been reunited as the Soviets removed obstacles, but twenty-one such cases remained between the United States and the USSR.

Novak tells us there are an estimated 200,000 Armenians who want to leave the Soviet Union and 150,000 ethnic Germans. He reminds us that 370,000 Soviet Jews have requested papers from abroad and that some 11,000 persons have been refused permission to emigrate.

Of the obstacles posed by the Soviet government, he asks, again and again, *Why?* Why should a powerful government deny citizens the right to leave? Few Russians, Ukrainians, or Balts are ever allowed to leave. Permission is seldom granted. "Consider," he asks us, "the Estonian couple who, seeking asylum in Sweden, were forced to leave behind their two-year-old daughter, who lives now with a grandmother herself deprived of employment. *"Why?"* he insists. "A great power could soften the crying of a two-year-old, allowing her now to join her parents, without any damage to its security, gaining honor for its open ways."

Socialism does not require that walls be built to keep people inside. Some socialist countries of Eastern Europe have less restrictive, less onerous policies. "Think it over," Novak urges the Soviet Union and the most repressive states of Eastern Europe. Arbitrary administrative obstacles that deny fathers the right to see sons, that deny wives the opportunities to join their husbands, ethnics the right to join their conationals—all such serve little purpose. A great nation does not need such restrictions.

Novak does not evade or understate the pervasive man-made obstacles to human contact created by the Soviets. He discusses them with candor but without anger. He seeks to explain and persuade, and though he has not succeeded—yet—in persuading the Russians, he persuades the reader of the utility of such meetings and conversations. "Our aim," Novak emphasizes, "is to help real people. We must keep their faces in mind as we approach the final decisions on the proposals now before us."

Novak believes there were three significant achievements at the compliance review at Bern: certain persons were actually helped, the review of compliance underscored the seriousness of the Helsinki commitment, and, finally, Novak believes that out of such meetings there is developing, incrementally, "a common European conscience."

Perhaps. It is not clear that the leaders and representatives of the Soviet Union will share a common conscience even if they speak a common language. And yet, why does the Soviet Union sign agreements such as the Helsinki Accords? Is it only because they seek tangible benefits—say, most-favored-nation status—and do not feel threatened by agreeing to provisions they will not implement? Soviet leaders have demonstrated again and again they are not much concerned with world opinion, but neither are they indifferent to it. At Bern they made clear they would rather amend the accords than be found in violation. Clearly, they cultivate the *impression* they share Western values. The Soviet government is not willing—yet—to practice the restraint required. But it is interesting that, unlike the Nazis or Fascists, the Soviets make a standard practice of affirming basic Western values rather than disputing them. This enables them to claim allegiance to "our flag"—a practice that strengthens them and confuses us. But it also keeps before that government the vision of free people in a free society.

Whatever the Soviet purpose or practices, it is important that we who do take seriously the Helsinki commitments reflect on their meaning and test our own compliance. It strengthens our commitment and understanding. It is good to be reminded that "humane values are deeper than politics and ideology; they are, in fact, their sole justification."

And it is gratifying to know that the United States was represented at Bern with such clarity, humanity, and realism. Our debt to Novak is large; part of it can be discharged by taking the time to read these speeches.

PART ONE
Preview

1
Assignment in Bern

It was only in December 1985 that I began to hear that I might be appointed to head the U.S. delegation to Bern. My calendar for the spring was already so crowded that I half wished the appointment would not come through. Thinking, however, of the members of my family (and the millions of kinfolk of other American families) behind the Iron Curtain, I knew such service to be a duty owed to them and an undeserved privilege.

Six weeks later, once the appointment seemed certain (and as the formal paperwork ground onward), the huge task of preparation hit me like a truck. Trips to Europe to consult with our allies would be necessary. Breaking precedent, the State Department and I also offered to meet in advance with the Soviets either in Europe or here. They suggested Moscow and we agreed; so that meant another long trip.

In addition, I needed to meet with the Helsinki Commission of the Congress, with the State Department, and with the leaders of the nongovernmental organizations (NGOs) concerned with peoples behind the Iron Curtain; these marvelous human rights activists are extraordinary sources of detailed information on general situations and particular cases. All the work I had planned to do during April and May, when the Bern meeting would take place, had to be compressed into February and March. It was a furious time.

To help the reader grasp what I had to learn, I offer below an account of my thinking during this period, before reaching Bern. This includes a syndicated column, prepared for March 14, and my advance testimony a few days later before the Helsinki Commission of the Congress. They should help establish some of the necessary background.

There is always some tension between Congress and the executive branch, and I soon learned that an ambassador has an urgent diplomatic task to perform in his home country even before departing for overseas. Meanwhile, there was a great deal of skepticism among human rights activists about the entire Helsinki process (which Jeane Kirkpatrick describes in her introduction to this volume).

Expectations for the Bern meeting were universally low. Realism *demanded* low expectations—neither the Ottawa (spring 1985) nor the Budapest (autumn 1985) meetings on kindred "basket three" subjects had led to harmony or final documents—but I judged right away that the United States ought to set the standard high. At the very least, the Bern meeting ought to vindicate the Helsinki process. It ought also to test the new sounds coming from Moscow about "a new spirit of cooperation" in humanitarian affairs—and to insist upon deeds, not words. But the main task, I thought, was to restore credibility to the Helsinki process, in the face of so many doubters. "This process is at least *something*," was my judgment; "let's make it work as best we can."

Perhaps, as in a novel, the reader should also receive here a sense of the larger drama. In the end, on the last day, we were to face a document in Bern that the State Department and I judged too weak for the United States to sign. Our withholding of consent dashed hopes for a consensus, which a skeptical press had begun to predict and to celebrate. Our delegation had had as much to do with moving the process of reaching consensus forward as any. But our eye had been fixed throughout on performance, not words. We judged the proposed words, once these were all assembled in one document on May 27, too weak. I especially thought that some of them were likely to come back to haunt us in the future. We had hoped for a break-through in the number of cases solved. We had hoped for Soviet willingness to agree to a stronger document. But we could honestly report no significant movement. And we judged that, as of the end of May, Soviet society was showing signs of greater closure, not open-ness. Soviet performance after the April 25 disaster at Chernobyl had been a scandal. Thousands of Ukrainians in the United States were frantic about the condition of their relatives within wind range of the still-leaking nuclear facility, but could not get through to them by telephone or learn truthful news about the situation from officials. I did not cherish the thought of coming back to the United States with a faulty document, about which I had serious doubts.

In Bern, we had asked for openness. At Bern, there were few signs of it: on the contrary. That is why, to the shock of a great many, the United States said no to the document at Bern. Skeptics who thought that U.S. delegations would continue to sign even poor documents, just for the sake of continuing the process, were also shocked. In many cases, such skeptics were happily shocked, since what they wanted most was integrity of words and actions. They saw that the United States meant what it said. Our delegation did as we had said we'd do. The shock was long-lasting.

I was personally extremely sorry to have to say no, not only because of the overwhelming barrage of hostile criticism that refusal brought down on me but, even more, because I more than anyone had wanted to coax the Soviets into greater and more rapid movement toward an open society. It is fanciful to think that my words at Bern— and perhaps the shock of our refusal to sign—played even a small role in encouraging General Secretary Gorbachev in the campaign of *glasnost* (openness) that he launched later on that summer. The reasons for his so doing were, no doubt, internal to the Soviet Union. Nonetheless, the United States by then was on record encouraging him to move in that direction. We had supplied concepts for expressing it and outlined some of the underlying forces in contemporary life that make "openness" the best, even the necessary, policy. This was the argument I had from the first intended to make at Bern, and did make. Here is how it began, in print and before the U.S. Congress in March of 1986.

2
On Human Contacts:
A Turning Point?

Beginning April 2, the nations of Europe (East and West), Canada, and the United States will send representatives to meet for eight weeks in Bern, Switzerland, for the next round of the "Helsinki process" discussions on security and cooperation in Europe. The subject in Bern will be human contacts—family reunification and visitation, the right to travel freely, cultural and athletic and professional contacts, the rights of religious institutions and associations, and the like. President Reagan has asked me to head the U.S. delegation, and, accordingly, I have traveled to visit European capitals, including Moscow, for advance consultations.

While in Moscow, I met with the "divided spouses"—men and women unable for years to join their husbands and wives in the United States. They are uncommonly beautiful and courageous persons. They have taken much hope from the promise of President Reagan and Secretary General Mikhail Gorbachev last November that there will be a new "spirit of cooperation on humanitarian affairs." Just three weeks ago, at the twenty-seventh Congress of the Communist Party USSR, the secretary general spoke anew of this "spirit of cooperation." The divided spouses—and millions of others—await eagerly the new actions that will give this spirit concrete reality.

Like Secretary General Gorbachev, my counterpart in the Soviet delegation, Yuri Kashlev, is in his early fifties. This new generation in its fifties will be responsible for human contacts from now through the end of this century, some fifteen years or so. In what ways will the flow of human contacts between East and West be better in the year 2000 than they are today? If this new generation begins in a new spirit, backed up by new deeds, much is possible.

About one in every ten Americans has roots in the nations of the Warsaw Pact. So when citizens of the United States show concern for human contacts among the peoples within their lands of origin, this is

---

Syndicated column, March 21, 1986.

not just a matter of politics. It is a family matter. For millions of Americans, the territories of the Soviet Union and other Central or Eastern European lands are their ancestral *rodina,* or homeland. If and when Secretary General Gorbachev visits the United States in 1986, he will find here millions of his "countrymen."

Yet life is unfair to such Americans today. Unlike their fellow citizens with roots in Italy, France, Africa, or Asia, they alone cannot freely visit their families in their places of origin or have these families freely come and visit them. This constraint seems so unnecessary. Why among all the places on the globe is there an "iron curtain" only in Europe? It does not have to be.

Often in the past, Soviet delegations have pointed out that there are "differences" between our systems. But *why* are there such differences? It is not enough to assert that differences exist. Reasons must also be given.

These reasons cannot be located merely in ideology. One can read the texts of Marx and Lenin in three or four different ways and apply them to human contacts in a way far different from the way the USSR does today. If a leader of the USSR wanted to decree different policies for human contacts than those now in force, he could find many texts in Marx to support such changes.

So the real reasons must lie elsewhere. Perhaps they lie in the Soviet perception of techniques they must use, as they see it, in order to govern. Whatever their reasons, it is important soon to make these understandable to the world at large.

Surely, the laws of every nation are different. But the rule of law requires that the law be clearly known to all and that the reasons for it also be clearly known. For sound law is founded in human reason and is properly changed as reason discovers better ways to meet reason's own purposes. Thus does law progress in history. If we are to keep our eyes fixed on how the situation of human contacts can be better in this world fifteen years from now than today, we must try incessantly to bring it into the full light of clear and reasonable law.

All the participants at Bern will hope that the new "spirit of cooperation in humanitarian affairs," including human contacts, will lead to new action on individual cases now causing personal anguish and to new procedures for making the handling of general classes of such cases lightsome, easy, regular, and routine.

Imagine the possibility that by the year 2000, the symbol of disrupted human contacts, the Berlin Wall that now extends like the Great Wall of China through the heart of Europe, were to come down. Imagine that human contacts were to flow more freely, as they do between all the other civilized parts of the globe. What a transforma-

7

tion of human contacts that would portend! That is an object worthy of the striving of the new generation of Soviet leaders now in their fifties.

The people of the United States are drawn from everywhere on this planet. A sizable minority of them—more than 20 million strong—have the closest possible ties with the USSR and the other nations of Eastern Europe. These are ties of roots and origins, of culture and of families. These are ties of history and affection. It is sad to see them so needlessly disrupted, disjointed, and irregular, as they are at present.

The peoples of the United States are also, whether the Soviets recognize this or not, a Biblical people. Every chapter in the Bible is about individual persons and their free acts of will. In one chapter King David is loyal to his Lord, in another unfaithful. So much hinges on individual will. That is why individuals are of such importance to the peoples of the Bible. It is not states alone that draw their love and attention but the fate of every single individual person.

To their credit, the USSR and its allies are signatories to the Helsinki Accords and the agreements reached later in Madrid. These agreements brilliantly defend the rights of individuals. There is already, then, a great deal in the "common law" of European nations, duly ratified. The question, alas, is still open about how well these agreements are to be kept in fact. Here is where great changes may yet come. Must come.

Europe is a great single civilization, nourished by the spiritual roots of Judaism and Christianity, in both Eastern and Western branches. The security of Europe rests on the degree of cooperation among its peoples, and upon the freedom and ease of the human contacts among the families, individuals, and associations that make up these peoples. Bern could be a turning point in global relations. Modest though its efforts be, it could be like that small portion of a panoramic battlefield, as described in Leo Tolstoy's *War and Peace*, on which the whole tide of battle turned. When I described Bern in this way in Moscow, my Soviet counterpart replied that the very building we were meeting in was described by Tolstoy in that novel. "Perhaps I felt his spirit in the walls," I replied.

Bern is a good place to put the new "spirit of cooperation" into deeds.

3
Prospects for Bern

MR. CHAIRMAN: I appreciate this opportunity to appear before you and this commission to discuss preparations for the Bern Experts' Meeting on Human Contacts. The very idea for the Bern meeting originated with this commission and in large part was carried through by your persistence. And contributions from the commission and its staff have so far been a large part of my education for Bern. I am grateful to all of you for this chance to serve my country.

I would like first to share some conclusions from recent consultation trips, on which Sam Wise of this commission's staff was of immense value. He seems to know everyone. His knowledge of the history of the "Helsinki process" seems unmatched. These trips have given me some appreciation of the spirit in which our NATO allies, the neutrals, and the Soviet Union are approaching this meeting.

Our allies agree that it is important for Bern to produce practical results. We define "practical results" precisely. We mean movement in specific individual cases. And we mean an improvement in the general conditions for cross-border human contacts by individuals and associations. In addition, a successful meeting entails a careful review of the record of how commitments of the Commission on Security and Cooperation in Europe (CSCE) have so far been implemented. Only through such a review can we explore ways by which the record might be improved in the future.

As always, close coordination among the NATO delegations at Bern on substantive and procedural issues will be a prerequisite to achieving the necessary concensus.

Cooperation with the neutral and nonaligned states, including our Swiss hosts, is also important. There are many indications that these delegations have similar objectives. Their own deliberations have produced conclusions about the structure of and prospects for the Bern meeting that seem realistic. Most do not, for instance, put a premium on producing a new document. Good language on human

Testimony of Michael Novak before the Commission on Security and Cooperation in Europe, Congress of the United States, March 18, 1986.

contacts already exists in the Helsinki and Madrid documents. We do not suffer from a shortage of texts. What the world suffers from is inadequate implementation of already existing texts.

There are few illusions among our European allies and friends about the difficulties inherent in the Bern meeting. It is possible that the Soviet Union will adopt a negative approach, in keeping with a desire to get through the meetings with as little pain as possible. We are hopeful that our initiative to consult bilaterally beforehand and to encourage accelerated progress on human contacts will enhance the possibilities for a constructive meeting. The Soviets greeted us cordially in Moscow on March 14 and expressed gratitude that we had come all the way to Moscow. I cannot say that they expressed flexibility, but they were not inflexible. It is in their power to make many changes. The new generation of Soviet leaders may yet heed Secretary General Gorbachev's call for "a new spirit of cooperation in humanitarian affairs." We will work to help make that true.

Mr. Chairman, as requested, I offer comments on specific subjects.

Role of Nongovernmental Organizations

Since December, the State Department has engaged the nongovernmental organizations (NGOs) interested in Bern in an extensive series of consultations—by mail, by telephone, in small groups, and in a large public meeting March 6, at which I was privileged to share the platform with Michael Hathaway, the executive director of the CSCE staff. The response to this effort has produced an abundance of useful suggestions. Some high-quality written materials have been presented to us. These greatly facilitate our substantive preparations. They add to the ammunition in our briefing books for the actual work of the session. We anticipate a vigorous liaison and assistance effort by the U.S. delegation with NGOs who come to Bern. I hope that an officer of this commission will agree to be chairman of this liaison effort in Bern, keeping me in the closest possible touch with the NGOs. In addition, the department plans to keep those at home informed by a series of mailings during and after the meeting. It hopes to do even better in this than in the similar effort made during the Budapest Cultural Forum, which many NGOs have praised.

Appointment of Public Members

Experts' meetings like Bern were mandated at Madrid precisely to allow government experts from the thirty-five participating states to address CSCE-related issues in their areas of responsibility. The United States has always attached special importance, however, to citizen participation. In this spirit, the State Department asked me to serve as head of the delegation to Bern, and the department has tried hard to draw NGOs into the CSCE process. In addition, the department is exploring the possibility of appointing as an adviser to the delegation an authoritative representative of the NGO community. I hope very much that this comes to pass.[1] In Bern, we will need all the hands we can muster. We expect many citizens from all over Europe to come seeking our assistance. Many U.S. associations and private citizens are also coming to Bern. It is the responsibility of our delegation—on which I hope members of your staff will serve—to make sure that the concerns of NGOs and individual citizens are well reflected at Bern.

Public Diplomacy

We must also do all we can to increase awareness of CSCE. The State Department has asked me to do my best on this and, in particular, to write one or more op-ed pieces on the subject. I submit a copy of my first effort in this direction for the record. It expresses my own convictions as I undertake this new assignment. The department has also prepared a variety of written materials for the media and the public. As the Bern meeting draws near, these materials will be put into use by the State Department, the U.S. Information Agency, and our embassies overseas. I plan to seize many opportunities for interviews before and during the meeting to bring it into public consciousness and am deeply grateful for the hearing that this commission plans to hold on April 15, just as the meetings begin. The press adviser on the delegation will have instructions to be as active and cooperative with the media in Bern as possible. We are told that the European press in particular will be present in Bern in considerable force.

Soviet Charges

In Moscow, our Soviet counterparts told us that, when criticized, the Soviets intend to attack the United States and its allies for *our* alleged violations of the Helsinki Final Act. We will welcome their efforts to fault our system. Our system thrives on criticism, public discussion, and the systematic redress of grievances. We will hope their system becomes ever more open—even for its own good—to similar procedures. The agreements reached at Helsinki and Madrid bind every

11

signatory. It is not "interference in internal affairs," as the Soviets say, to hold one another to strict adherence to agreements commonly arrived at.

Conclusion

Meanwhile, I thank this commission for its extremely creative and constructive work down the years. As an American of central European background, of Slovak heritage, I am especially grateful for the concern it has shown for the fate of those one in ten of all American families whose roots lie in the nations of the Warsaw Pact. For all Americans, concern about human contacts with the "other half of Europe" are not so much a matter of politics as of family. Americans are Americans precisely because of the values embodied in the Helsinki Final Act. We cannot do otherwise than to make these values real and effective, for those portions of our families that do not at present enjoy their gentle sway. Thank you, Mr. Chairman, for all this commission has done to advance the universal desire for more humane human contacts in that vital part of the world, the dynamic continent of Europe, where security rests on the cooperation freely exercised among its peoples, associations, and individuals.

Note

1. Indeed, George Urban and William Korey were each accredited to the U.S. delegation in Bern and contributed their energy and wisdom.

PART TWO

Speeches in Bern:
April 3–May 27, 1986

4
Bern: Purpose and Background

The Preparatory Session

Most of our delegation flew out from Dulles airport in Washington on Easter Sunday evening, March 30, 1986, bound for Geneva, where a van awaited to drive us through the snow to Bern. The views of the mountains and along the lake were breathtaking, even under an overcast, intermittently snowy sky. Arriving in Bern shortly after noon, we went fairly speedily to work. Our offices were to be at the U.S. embassy across town, at some distance from the beautiful hotel downtown, the Bellevue Palace, where the Experts' Meeting was to convene. (The Bellevue was made so secure by Swiss police during those eight weeks that some called it the best-protected building in Europe.) We began with a scheduled meeting with our NATO allies at a meeting room attached to our embassy. Also, I began work immediately on the speech to be given on the first working day, Wednesday, of the preparatory session.

Each meeting in the Helsinki process must establish its own work program and division of labors. Thus, each is preceded by a preparatory session of a duration specified in advance—in our case, two weeks. These meetings are important. They decide the official order of proceeding, the calendar of activities, and the distribution of emphasis. The Soviet delegation typically fights hard to block discussion of certain matters. It uses byzantine discussions of procedures to give it as favorable a playing field as possible for its later substantive purposes. In Bern, the objectives of the allies included one *sine qua non* and one *desideratum:* to reserve as much time for the review of compliance as possible (half the sessions or more) and, if possible, to increase the number of meetings open to the press and the public.

The United States wanted from the beginning to stress openness, but we had not at first planned to fight so hard for a larger number of open meetings. Since CSCE tradition was on the side of closed meetings (except for the formal public opening and —a first at Ottawa—the formal closing speeches), not much progress could be expected. But we did want modest progress. And we decided to place great stress upon that point, as our seeming goal. Most of all, we wanted at least half the sessions during the subsequent six weeks to be set aside for a review of compliance. And we wanted much more time to discuss family and religious issues, whereas the Warsaw Pact nations preferred long discussions of sports, tourism, and travel for scientific or cultural purposes.

By the end of the preparatory session, the thirty-five nations must reach consensus on a written agenda. Thus, the last day, I had my first taste of an all-night meeting, Soviet-style. At the closing hour, the negotiating teams (three delegations from each side closeted in a small room, on opposite sides of a green felt-covered table) were nowhere near agreement. This, I was told, is normal CSCE procedure. The official clock is simply "stopped" by consensus just before midnight, so that the officially prescribed closing hour will not be violated. The Soviets remain stubborn. They continue to argue hard. Reasonableness is not necessary to their case; they change reasons as needed. Moscow has set their goals, and they fight as if Siberia threatened them if they should fail.

At Bern, we estimated that Moscow did not want a discordant opening. We held firm. Thus, after tedious and almost endless Leninist negotiations, the Soviet delegation agreed somewhere around 4 A.M. to a schedule that gave us plenty of time for a review of compliance.

On the proposal to allow for a few more open meetings, the Soviets had to stand against it alone, in effect to veto it. They conceded only that the open final speeches could go for two plenary sessions, if necessary. At a press conference, I defended the Soviet right to do as they did, under the Helsinki rules. While regretting their unwillingness to move toward greater openness, I said it was not quite right to call their negative vote a veto, since consensus is the norm for all Helsinki meetings. Later, I was glad I had defended the USSR on this point; we ourselves would stand alone against consensus six weeks later, on the final day.

A successful preparatory meeting behind us, we were eager to get to the substantive questions. Besides, we were glad that the focus had fallen upon openness so early.

Terrorist Actions

Regarding the climate in which our work began, it may be useful for the reader to recall the many terrorist acts of the winter of 1985–1986. On the preceding October 7–10, 1985, the seizure of the *Achille Lauro*, its rescue, and the forced landing of the hijackers' plane had shown

16

the world high drama. Later in the "winter of terror in Europe," three bombs went off in Paris, February 3–5, wounding twenty-one. On February 28, Olof Palme was assassinated in Stockholm as he and his wife were walking home from the theater. During March 24–25, Libya attacked the U.S. Navy sailing in the Gulf of Sidra; at least two Libyan ships were sunk and inland radar sites disabled. On March 29, seven Arabs were wounded in a bombing in West Berlin. Four days later, just as we were assembling in Bern, a bomb exploded in a TWA airliner on a flight between Rome and Athens. Four Americans were killed, nine others wounded. In West Berlin on April 5, a disco frequented by Americans was bombed and an American serviceman and a Turkish woman died. On April 14, U.S. F-111s bombed Tripoli and Benghazi, Libya.

Often during these days, intelligence reports put Bern (and other U.S. embassies in Europe) on special alert. Ambassadors of three friendly nations, visiting me in my hotel across town (where no guards were in evidence), urged me strongly to move to the protected Bellevue Palace. Querying Washington, I was told to do so.

Ambiance of the Meetings

A word about the ambiance of the meetings may also be helpful. To get into the Bellevue, every person had to walk a gauntlet of heavily armed, black leather–coated Swiss policemen who politely asked to see official badges. An electronic device inside submitted these badges to scrutiny, briefcases and parcels went through a screening device, and all persons also had to walk through a detector. At various checkpoints, at doorways, for example, other persons asked to see official badges. Woe to anyone, no matter how well known to the guards, who forgot to bring a badge (as everybody did—once). The Swiss obey orders, even while showing graciousness. They had obviously been told: "no exceptions." There were none.

To the left of the great lobby lay the princely ballroom, decked out with thirty-five national flags, with tables formed in a long rectangle around a bright open space. Around the outside of the tables two chairs were placed for representatives of each delegation, plus three more for two Swiss executive officers of the meeting and the chairman of the day. Behind the representatives at the table were seats for additional staff.

No one could speak until recognized by the chair. Rather than addressing one another, each delegation by rule addressed the chairman, thus avoiding direct confrontation and ensuring order. In referring to other speakers, custom holds that one must always use the

17

formal expression "the distinguished delegate of . . .," which had the effect of ruling out any *un*distinguished delegates, we told one another, and the useful purposes of preventing personal acrimony and defusing any potential personalization of formal arguments.

To the left of the entrance was a two-story enclosure for the translators into the six official languages (English, French, German, Italian, Spanish, and Russian). The great windows to the outdoors had been heavily covered for security. The room was sparkling clean; the waxed hardwood floors shone blond under bright lights. The table was so large around that one's colleagues opposite seemed quite far away. The nations were arranged alphabetically.

To gain access to the translators and to the sound system, each speaker pressed a button on his or her microphone before speaking and afterwards. Earphones were provided for translation. To be translated accurately at all, one had to speak slowly. Thus, readers of the speeches should "listen" to them as if reading them aloud internally, since the style of oral discourse is necessarily different from that of written essays, and the drama of oral delivery is more different still. My own speech came very early in the proceedings. I had worked hard on it.

5
Peace, Cooperation, and Security

APRIL 3, 1986

MR. CHAIRMAN, DISTINGUISHED DELEGATES: Representing my government, permit me to thank and to commend our Swiss hosts for the excellence of their hospitality, for their forethought, and for these lovely, practical facilities. Few of us could offer facilities at once so beautiful and so homelike—so much in human scale.

Representing my delegation, permit me to say how glad our veterans of CSCE meetings feel—those who have been present since the beginning—to join again with so many colleagues in the important work of this meeting. (In some respects, meetings of CSCE are themselves a kind of "family reunification.")

In my own name, allow me to say what a privilege it is to be associated with the vital work of the CSCE—which is on the very frontline of world concerns. To my mind this Helsinki process is the key international assemblage, the pivotal point.

In preparing for this meeting, we thought back to 1975 at the Helsinki Final Act, to 1980 when under President Jimmy Carter the Madrid Conference began, and to 1983 when under President Reagan and with basic continuity the Madrid Conference closed. In that same spirit of continuity our delegation begins it work today.

Much has changed in the world since 1975, since 1980, and even since 1983. We see a new revolution in the world of communications and in the technical means through which human contacts may be established independently of central controls. We see a new technology of personal computers, word processors, fiber optics, and satellites, which will free individual human beings to communicate with others around the world as never before. We foresee a world of small, portable, personal television sets and telephones, through which individual human beings will be able to establish contact with other human beings anywhere in the world.

Politically as well as technologically, we see a new world. Thus, we recognize that a new moment is at hand. In the past few years we have seen the appearance of a revitalized United States and Canada, a revitalized Western Europe, and even a revitalized Eastern Europe. We see a new, vigorous, young leader as the secretary general of the USSR and behind him a whole new generation of Soviet leaders, who in the years of their most intense activity will have responsibilities to meet before history, until the end of this century.

Therefore, we listened with great interest and expectation to the words pronounced in Geneva by the secretary general concerning a spirit of cooperation in humanitarian affairs. We noted with hope and expectation when he repeated these same words, a new "humane and positive spirit" of cooperation in humanitarian affairs at the Twenty-seventh Congress in Moscow. These words may mark the beginning of a new era. Much depends on what is made of them in concrete reality.

Moreover, these words were recalled to me by President Reagan, by whose authority I serve here, when I had the privilege of a brief meeting with him just before departing for Bern. President Reagan asked me to communicate to you, and to the world, how important the normal human contacts of individuals and families are to the people of the United States. The people of the United States, he suggested, judge regimes by the quality of the human contacts they permit. And his words made me think that, initially, there is no need for harsh words, no need for public display. What is most important to the people of the United States is tangible improvement in the daily reality of many individual lives. What is important to us is the reality, much more than the words.

In preparing myself for this meeting, I read over some of the speeches given during the preparatory meetings at Madrid. These meetings are important to us, because our colleagues at the Madrid Conference were the founding fathers of this meeting in Bern. They often spoke of the need to proceed without illusions, on the firm basis of reality, while making a clear review of the record, a record that had given them so many disappointments since 1975. Moreover, in the words of Ambassador Max Kampelman, my predecessor as head of the U.S. delegation in Madrid, our colleagues in Madrid reminded one another often that they should choose the path of reason, proceed with pragmatism, and keep their eyes fixed upon concrete improvements in the real lives of individuals.

For example, in his concluding speech in Madrid on July 15, 1983, after reviewing the six improvements Madrid added to the language about human contacts in the Helsinki Final Act, Ambassador Kampelman spoke these words:

> There was one additional step taken after months of debate and stalemate. The West believes that it is important to provide a forum after Madrid and before the next followup meeting for the issue of human contacts to be thoroughly explored at a meeting of experts attended by representatives

of all thirty-five countries. We look upon an experts' meeting as a means of providing an opportunity for further clarity and, perhaps, understanding among us all, so that by the time of the next followup meeting this issue might be less of an irritant.

The government of Switzerland shared our belief and invited the participating states to an experts' meeting to deal with human contacts during April 1986. This was finally accepted by the Soviet Union. A late date was selected so that we will have time to examine how the six new provisions in the Madrid agreement will have been complied with. We look upon this meeting as an important development.

Thus, our founding fathers at Madrid looked upon the Bern meetings as a potential turning point. This becomes particularly clear when we reflect on one of the first words to appear in the Madrid document. That word is détente. Already in 1980 détente was beginning to lose its clarity and its positive ring. It is a word that, if it has any meaning left to it at all today, has three parts: peace, cooperation, and security. Each one of these three realities depends principally upon—is constituted by—the quality of human contacts.

Consider peace. What is peace? Peace is the situation in which human contacts are freely arrived at. Peace is the dynamic of ordered tranquillity, as St. Augustine put it—an order that is lawlike, brotherly, free, uncoerced.

What is cooperation? Cooperation means not only that human beings maintain contact with one another, but also that they work together. They give one another common assistance, toward purposes freely arrived at by each of them. Cooperation implies liberty and choice. Cooperation must be freely given; it is a precious form of human contact.

What is security? Security is achieved when human beings live in mutual contact without fear, in freedom, without threat. Peace, cooperation, and security—at the heart of each lies the concept of human contacts. Only by the quality of these human contacts do we know whether we have peace, cooperation, and security. These three are constituted by free human contacts, chosen without fear, freely entered into.

We Americans look toward Europe for our spiritual roots. We see that for centuries Europe, East and West, has grown as two branches of one same root. We see Europe entering into a new era of closer contact constituted by a new technology and a new politics. Those who would prepare themselves for this new era must make decisions now about the quality of the human contacts that will characterize European life by the time this century ends.

THE WORLD BEYOND BERN: TERROR IN EUROPE

On Wednesday evening, April 2, we learned that a bomb had exploded that day on TWA Flight 840 from Rome to Athens. Alberto Ospino had a window seat in row ten. A bomb went off under him, blowing a nine-foot hole in the plane. As the cabin decompressed, he and three persons in the row behind were sucked out. The bodies of Ospino, Demetra Stylianopoulos, her daughter Maria Klug, and her infant granddaughter Demetra Klug were later found in southern Greece. In all, four American passengers were killed, nine others injured.

Already in its descent to Athens, the plane was at a relatively low altitude. Had the bomb exploded earlier, catastrophic decompression would probably have destroyed the plane. The jet instead managed to land safely in Athens.

Hours later, a unit of the Arab Revolutionary Cells associated with terrorist Abu Nidal claimed responsibility in Beirut. The same group had earlier been held responsible for the December 1985 Rome and Vienna airport massacres that killed eighteen.

Italian Interior Minister Oscar Luigi Scalfaro said April 3 that May Elias Mansur, a known terrorist and "expert in explosives," was believed to have planted the bomb on the flight's Cairo-to-Athens leg, before flying to Beirut on another airline.

Then, we learned on Sunday morning, April 6, that the night before a bomb had killed two persons in a West Berlin discotheque frequented by U.S. servicemen. Sgt. Kenneth T. Ford and Nermin Haney, a Turkish woman, were killed in the early morning blast that injured 230, including 50 American soldiers and their relatives.

The Red Army Faction of West Germany, its offshoot the Holger Meins Commando (which also claimed to have assassinated Olof Palme a month earlier), and a previously unknown Arab group claimed responsibility for the bombing.

Citing strong evidence of Libyan sponsorship, the United States indicated it was considering military retaliation against Libya and urged European allies to expel Libyan diplomats. France immediatly expelled four Arab diplomats, including two Libyans, thought to be planning attacks on Americans. On Wednesday, April 9, West Germany expelled two Libyan diplomats for "impermissible activities," and Qaddafi warned the United States that, if attacked, he would order Arab and other radical groups to attack "American targets all over the world."

6

Open Plenary Meetings and the Public

APRIL 7, 1986

MR. CHAIRMAN: Permit me to propose two principles that might prove useful in our present considerations: the principle of openness and the principle of compromise. The first follows from our subject matter, the second from our method of consensus.

Our delegation, it is obvious, represents the people of the United States, an immigrant people, drawn from every quarter of the world, a people nearly all of whose roots lie elsewhere. One out of ten Americans, for example, has at least one grandparent from the lands of Central and Eastern Europe. Therefore, the interests of millions of American families—part in America, part in Eastern Europe—are deeply involved in what happens to the Eastern branches of their families. Their interest is not so much political, and not so much ideological, as it is familial. Whatever happens to their relatives is a family affair.

In addition, for the people of the United States the business of the states is a public business. Governance is by consent of the governed. Therefore, about laws made, agreements entered into, and actions taken by the state, the people have a right to know. My delegation, for example, is directly answerable to the people. Even before coming here, I was summoned before Congress to give an account of what I *intended* to say and do here, even before I did it. Everything I do or say here will later be subject to the judgment of our people. Most of the delegations assembled here are similarly accountable.

From such a background, Mr. Chairman, and fellow delegates, you will understand why our delegation is in favor of maximum openness in as many of our plenary sessions as possible. Our distinguished colleague, the head of the Soviet delegation, for whom I have already learned both a professional and a personal esteem, mentioned last Thursday that we should proceed in a businesslike manner and that this in his judgment requires closed meetings. We understand and respect his point of view. Nonetheless, our own tradition leads us to the opposite conclusion. Precisely in *order* to be businesslike, our meetings ought to be open. Our business is the public's business;

states are formed to serve the people, not the reverse. Therefore, Mr. Chairman, it would better reflect the distinctive ideals of our own democracies if most of our meetings in Bern—at least a large proportion of our plenary meetings—were open to the public, as are the meetings of the houses of representatives, senates, parliaments, and public commissions in our several nations.

We recognize that others disagree with us. And in such cases, besides openness, democratic peoples such as ours cherish another principle: a willingness to compromise for the common good. Therefore, with due respect for CSCE traditions and their demonstrated record of gradual development, we are not here asking for complete openness at all meetings. We ask openness only for a portion of the plenary sessions, not for the working groups, which some among our colleagues would like to see established. If such working groups do come into existence, our proposal would mean open sessions for considerably less than half the conference as a whole.

You have a right, fellow delegates, to remind us of objections to our point of view. It is often said, for example, that public meetings make effective progress less likely. Yet the most effective negotiations in the CSCE process do not (and should not) take place in plenary or on the floor. And, if there is a compromise on working groups, most of the sessions of the conference will in any case be closed. As for the relatively few open meetings we are requesting, in our experience the public has a careful conscience. It is always best to trust the public. Over time the public sees through falsity and propaganda, has sound judgment, and shows great common sense. We trust our public. Our public trusts us—or else we are gone. These meetings in Bern will be all the more businesslike, if all of us are accountable to the public.

The reason why this is so is plain. What is the subject matter of this meeting? Human contacts. Does not the public know better than we the full range of human contacts, the full pain of broken or prevented human contacts? Do not all of us hear from the public every day by telephone and letter and photograph? Since my name was announced for this post, I have been weighed down by hundreds of sad stories, one after another. I carry with me to this conference a mail bag heavy with evidence of pain.

Does not the public know about sports? What would sports be without an eager public? Does not the public know about tourism? Has not every member of the public a family, a spouse, children, an aged parent, a birthplace, or a cemetery in one *rodina* or another in which the bones of grandparents lie? The public carries a huge burden of tearful knowledge about human contacts in our time. The public may know more than we about the proper subject of this meeting. Here the public supplies the experts. We are merely students of phenomena, whose millions of hidden veins of suffering we are humanly incapable of knowing.

Mr. Chairman, esteemed colleagues, there is no other subject matter that more touches the public, more belongs to the public, and is better known to the public, than "human contacts" (and their untimely interruption). No other subject matter—not even human rights, with their institutions, due process, and formal procedures—is so close to the people as are matters such as family, freedom of personal movement, sports, tourism, and social belief in God.

Our delegation concludes from these reflections that the Bern procedures after April 15, with full respect for the important precedents that have accumulated over the ten years of this process, ought to be more open than any other meetings in the CSCE process. The subject matter itself demands it. The public has an interest in knowing what we say and how we say it, concerning matters even closer to them than to us—to *their* human contacts, *their* human possibilities, *their* loves, *their* private hopes. What have government officials to say about love?

I repeat, Mr. Chairman, our delegation is willing to compromise, for the common good, in this assembly of many nations and many philosophies. All we ask is that our meetings on such a subject, closer to the public than to ourselves, be not only as open as earlier meetings in the CSCE tradition but somewhat more so. We look for a reasoned compromise, which each of us will be proud to take to our diverse publics.

THE WORLD BEYOND BERN: LIBYA

On Monday, April 14, as representatives at Bern struggled to agree on agendas and procedures before the meeting's official opening on Tuesday, American warplanes bombed terrorist targets in Tripoli and Benghazi, Libya. President Reagan ordered the strikes both to retaliate for the terrorist bombing of a West Berlin discotheque that had killed an American soldier nine days earlier and to deter future terrorist attacks.

At 2 A.M. local time, Air Force F-111s from Great Britain and carrier-based Navy bombers from the Mediterranean Sea raided five targets in Libya's "terrorist infrastructure." The planes stationed in Britain had to fly 2,800 nautical miles down the eastern Atlantic and through the Strait of Gibraltar. The seven-hour trip required four midair refuelings.

Electronic jamming planes from Britain and A-7 and F-18 attack aircraft from the U.S.S. America and U.S.S. Coral Sea jammed Libya's defenses and destroyed Libyan anti-aircraft batteries. The F-111s, joined by A-6 bombers from the carriers, attacked from the sea at altitudes as low as 350 feet to drop laser-guided "smart" bombs. While the A-6s raided a military airfield and command barracks at Benghazi, the F-111s bombed Qaddafi's headquarters outside of Tripoli, as well as the Sidi Bilal seaport and a military airport. One F-111 and its crew were lost in the ten-minute raid.

With the exception of Great Britain, the European allies of the United States publicly condemned the raid, as did almost all third world nations. Mikhail Gorbachev denounced the action and weakly reassured Qaddafi that the Soviet Union "firmly intends to fulfill its commitments in terms of further strengthening Libya's defense capability."

Although terrorist acts began to diminish significantly, the decrease did not appear at first. Within three days, a bomb was found in a pregnant woman's luggage as she attempted to board an El AL 747 at Heathrow airport, and a U.S. diplomat's car in Tunis was firebombed.

THE FORMAL SESSION

After the virtually all-night meeting that allowed us to close the preparatory session by Tuesday afternoon, April 15, I returned to working on my speech for the first day of business on Wednesday. It was good that I did. At the splendid formal opening, a little Swiss girl in a flowered dress chose a scroll at random from a large basket; Swiss officials unrolled it and read out the name of the first chairman of the day—"the United States of America"—and then the little girl walked over to me to present a bouquet as the one fate had selected to open the Bern debates as chairman. This meant that all that day I would be in the chair, unable to work on my speech.

Another observation worth making: during the cocktail party at that same formal opening, I found myself talking with the leaders of the Soviet and Polish delegations, Yuri Kashlev and Jerzy Nowak (no relation!). We found ourselves discussing this question; How could strict societies such as Poland and the USSR deal with new technologies of communication such as personal computers? The discussion flowed easily among the three of us. I offered my own theory about the choice to be faced: either allow personal computers (with access to central data) or fall ever further behind. "Mind is the principle of progress," I said; "mind requires openness." We discussed television signals of the future that might be beamed into individual sets within one country from satellites of another, futuristic personal telephones that go through no central switchboard, and the like. A lecturer in communications courses at the academy of the Foreign Ministry in Moscow, Yuri Kashlev did not deny the power of the coming revolution in communications but acknowledged it as a serious problem. An affable and forthright man, given to chain-smoking Winston cigarettes, he had heretofore traveled extensively around the world (he had served in China, New York, and London) and beneath a casual exterior exhibited considerable sophistication. I judged that he was a strong backer of Gorbachev. He often said that the USSR would move toward a new kind of future.

The next day we got down to business. The daily grind of meetings began. Since the phrase "ordinary people," used in my maiden speech, became the most quoted phrase of the next six weeks, I suffered much teasing because of it. Some chided me that the Bern meeting would go down in history as "the experts meeting on ordinary people." It was a theme exactly suited to our subject and rooted in the Helsinki tradition. William Korey's little booklet on the Helsinki process, which I had read in preparation, had suggested it to me. It set, I thought, a good tone for the beginning.

7
Ordinary People:
The Dream and the Reality

APRIL 17, 1986

MR. CHAIRMAN: The people of the United States, through our delegation, would like to thank the people of Switzerland, and with them the Executive Secretary and his every single staff person, for the generosity, the open-heartedness and the perfection of the arrangements with which they have welcomed us.

In this city, at every turn, the virtues of the Swiss people are apparent: dignity; a striving for excellence; a love for intellect and the works thereof; an instinct for the beauty of God's mountains and the creativity of humankind. In this way, the ordinary people of Switzerland—their laws, their traditions, their habits of the heart—shed light upon our mandate: "to discuss the development of contacts among persons, institutions and organizations."

In which country of the world are contacts among persons, institutions and organizations developed to a higher art? In which are human contacts so international, open, orderly and warm? If all the world were Switzerland, the burden of our mandate would be light.

Nearly eleven years ago, the distinguished foreign secretary of the United Kingdom, then Sir Alec Douglas-Home, threw down a challenge: "If we do not improve the life of ordinary people at this conference," he said of Helsinki, "we shall be asked—and with justice—what all our fine words and diplomatic phrases have achieved." Ordinary people. If we do not improve the life of ordinary people, words are empty. There remains a darkness in which many millions cry.

Ordinary people are our subject here: ordinary people in their ordinariness—with their spouses, their children, their parents, their grandparents, their multiple relatives; the cemeteries where the bones of their ancestors lie and the shaded rooms in which their sick languish; their sports and travels; their friends and relatives blown abroad upon the winds of war and chance and choice; their professions; and the deepest convictions of their hearts.

Ordinary people are our theme. Our mandate is: to improve their lives—"to discuss the development of contacts"—that is, to seek improvement in their contacts with other human beings and to discern the impediments, obstacles, and barbed wire walls, the tangles of law and administrative breakdowns, which interrupt such contacts. We act in the name of peace, security, and cooperation in Europe, and these four go together: peace, security, cooperation, and ordinary people, in their ordinary human contacts.

What do ordinary people want? It is not so very much: ordinary liberty to do ordinary human things without any state standing in their way. This is a universal dream of all ordinary people everywhere. It is a dream embodied, codified, set down in clear words, and certified by thirty-five heads of state on the first day of August 1975, in Helsinki, Finland: Ordinary liberties for ordinary people.

The Dream

In Moscow last February 25, General Secretary Mikhail Gorbachev expressed a portion of this dream in a few brief "fundamental principles" in "the humanitarian sphere":

• broader contact between peoples for the purpose of learning about one another; reinforcement of the spirit of mutual understanding and concord in relations between them
• decision in a humane and positive spirit of questions related to the reunification of families, marriage and the promotion of contacts between people and between organizations

This is one nation's view of the universal dream. The dream is more powerful than the views of any nation, or of all nations. This dream does not originate in states and cannot be contained by states. It is endowed in ordinary people everywhere, by the deepest and most powerful endowment.

This is the dream that haunts our ever-ancient, ever-new European civilization. For Marxists as well as for democratic capitalists, for believers and unbelievers, for all who speak the languages of Europe, think the thoughts of Europe, and give evidence in their lives of the habits of Europe—for all these, the roots of European culture lie buried deep in these three convictions of Judaism and Christianity:

1. It is the vocation of Europeans (as of all humans) to change history, not merely to be passive before it.

2. To meet this vocation, every single human being has been created free and responsible, and is endowed with unalienable rights to pursue the vocation of human development to its fullest.

3. To protect these rights, governments are formed among men to improve the life of ordinary people, through the consent of ordinary people.

General Secretary Gorbachev speaks of a dialogue among "leaders of countries." It is also, far more deeply, a dialogue among the world's ordinary people. Everywhere, Europeans today seek the intellectual roots of our common humanity, our common roots, at the core of every European spirit.

This CSCE—this conference, this institution of no fixed abode, with no permanent staff and no permanent budget—is fashioning a new Europe, and persons of middling age—that is, most of us in this room—have in our care the nurturing of this Europe for the next fourteen years, until the year 2000, and on into the next, twenty-first century, with the hope that it might be the most creative of all human centuries.

Indeed, a new era in human contacts is already forming, through technology, which no government will be able to control. This technology is personal, designed to obey individual will: personal computers, word processors, video cassettes, portable hand-held telephones, and television communicators. It is now possible to control carbon paper through serial numbers; it is now possible to put padlocks on copiers. But it will not be possible for central authorities to control the new personal media. Those who try will enter obsolescence.

As we enter this new age, the test for every nation will be; Does it improve the life of ordinary people? Or does it enter slow decline?

The Reality

I have tried to sketch the dream that unites all delegations in this room. Now I must face the other way, toward reality. The reality, alas, is not like the dream.

Let me put the matter as gently as I can. About one American in ten has at least one family root in Central and Eastern Europe: some 23 million Americans. One part of their growing family tree spreads branches in America; part grows still in Europe. Along such family networks, through such human contacts—by letter and by telephone, by memory and sympathy, in ways both straight and indirect—come jolting shocks of reality.

Of all American citizens, those of Central and East European heritage find it most difficult to exercise freely the rights of human contact with their families abroad. Our fellow citizens, who spring from Swiss or French, Italian or Spanish, Irish or Norwegian—indeed from Latin American or African or Asian—stock, find almost no difficulties in exercising free and open contact with their families in their *rodina* of origin. Not so with us.

We hear pleas from relatives of ours in the Baltic states and Ukraine, among others, pleas from relatives of ours elsewhere in Eastern Europe, pleas from relatives of ours among Jews in several lands. We hear realities from thousands upon thousands who seek to visit, or to move abroad, according to the choices of their heart. To hear from such as these is to pass from dream to reality.

Let me say a word about how our delegation will proceed. The people of the United States are a Biblical people. Like the Bible itself, we think naturally in stories, in terms of individual cases, which are the foundation of the common law. From time to time, our delegation will, quite naturally, mention the individual cases of those whose dreams have not yet been realized.

In this context, my delegation honors the citizen monitors in so many countries, who took the words of the Helsinki Final Act with dreadful seriousness. These brave men and women—heroes to the entire human race—have bravely endured so much more than any of us to make the dreams of the Final Act the dramatic material of a new beginning. They have begun the task of making words of law deeds of flesh, of making dreams realities, of turning solemn international commitments into actual "decisions in a humane and positive spirit."

The people of the United States are also a family people. Families are dear to us, as are the multiplicity of freely chosen associations in which we live our daily lives. Our hearts are especially drawn to the divided spouses, separated from each other's arms for so many years. We are touched by family members, seeking to join that portion of their family tree they freely choose.

This is not the occasion for details. Suffice it to say that many letters and calls make us aware of greater pain than words will express. Perhaps the reality to which I speak is best expressed in the image President Reagan evoked in dispatching me to Bern—an image of the Great Wall through the heart of Europe, dividing Europe, symbolizing the rude interruption of normal human contacts. In the twenty-first century, will that wall stand? Will it be necessary? Will it remain, as an affront to dignity, to liberty, and to the ordinary human contacts of ordinary human beings?

It is said at times that Europe is today divided by two philosophies, two different social systems, two different images of how human contacts should be exercised. On one side, it is said, are those who believe that human contacts ought to be steered, controlled by the state, for the interests of the state. On the other side, it is said, are those who believe that human contacts ought to spring from the soul of every individual person, from choice, from will, from self-determination: human contacts of ordinary people, by ordinary people, for

31

ordinary people. Two different social systems, two different philoso-phies.

Suppose this description is true. What is never addressed is, *Why*. How are these two systems justified? In the night, in the words of Chekhov, one hears the sobbing of a child. "Why?" the child asks.

Our mandate is to "discuss the development of contacts among persons, institutions, and organizations." We will, therefore, discuss laws, regulations, habits, and ways of acting. We will discuss these both in dream and in reality. We must discuss them with hope for concrete improvements in the lives of ordinary citizens—in the words of General Secretary Gorbachev, new "decisions in a humane and positive spirit." And we must discuss them face to face with reality. Many ordinary people suffer in the darkness. Our delegation intends to hear and to voice their pain.

Above all, we look to a better Europe soon. An open Europe. A Europe without a wall. Europe free from fear; acting out in reality the peace, security, and cooperation to which the Helsinki Final Act and the Madrid Concluding Document committed all of us. We look to the scrupulous application of those commitments. All our nations have publicly affixed their names to them.

We thank every delegation for dreaming this dream with us, facing reality with us, so that all cooperating together, Europe may experience another, morally fuller, renaissance.

8
Right of Reply: On Terrorism
APRIL 18, 1986

Yesterday, Mr. Chairman, two delegations raised the question of terrorism. Because I was the chairman of the day, and because their references were oblique, it seemed appropriate to wait until today to make a comment.

One does not have to agree with Thomas Hobbes to note that without civilization, there is only terrorism: nothing but brute power, murder, and fear. Civilization begins with triumph over terror.

Although the Helsinki Final Act and the Madrid Concluding Document affirm several penetrating points about terrorism, terrorism is not the subject of our mandate at Bern. By contrast, though, civilization is a theme important to us, because civilization is the precondition for authentically human contacts. Civilization is the rule of law substituted for the rule of terror. Since it is a work of reason, civilization consists in layer upon layer of defenses against terror. The right to defend civilization against terror is inherent in civilization. The right to defend civilization against terror is permitted by international law; it is commanded by the moral law.

During our first weekend in Bern, on the evening of April 5, as we were just meeting one another, scores of young men and women in Berlin were also meeting. It was a weekend. They were dancing. Like young people everywhere, they were carefree, relaxed, and happy.

So also, a few days earlier, were the passengers on the TWA airliner flying smoothly over Athens. These normal human contacts among peaceful citizens of several states were suddenly jolted by explosions. At 12,000 feet, from out of the blasted fuselage three adults and one infant were sucked to their deaths. In Berlin, the dancing was stopped by horror, the same horror that surrounds all civilized people today, as once it did centuries ago.

Let me return to my original theme. Centuries ago, both in ancient times and in medieval times, the cities of Europe had their origins in a

---

On the night of April 14, U.S. F-111s bombed Libya. Two Warsaw Pact delegations used the occasion to turn criticism of terrorism onto the United States. The chairmanship of the plenary sessions rotated daily. The policy of our delegation was to answer every substantive attack upon the United States. Most other delegations followed the same policy with regard to their own countries.

determined battle against terrorism. These walled cities, often built above cliffs, were islands of safety within a countryside preyed upon by brigands and marauders.

In the coming renaissance of Europe, Europe will again break the grip of terrorism. Europe will rise free from terrorism. Europe will do so because of the resolution and determination of all its citizens. The citizens of the United States will be at their side. The citizens of Europe, of Canada, and of the United States now bear the burden of this struggle, not because we chose to, but because it was thrust upon us. Innocent civilians in innocent surroundings have the right to be free from fear. And they will be.

Soviet Accusation

After the first round of opening speeches, the meeting entered upon the review of compliance with the Helsinki Accords and the follow-up Madrid Concluding Document. During our trip to Moscow, Soviet officials had pointed to a thick binder packed, they said, with the "ammunition" that they intended to use against the United States in case we should criticize their record on human rights. They had already begun to use this tactic in Ottawa the preceding year (a tactic, which, under Gorbachev, they were clearly trying to perfect), where it was very effectively rebutted by the Americans. I was delighted to learn of these intentions, since, before Ottawa, the Soviets had always argued that no state had the right to "interfere" in the "internal affairs" of any other. To drop that claim and to engage in mutual criticism was a major concession to the principle of fresh and open argument. This concession led naturally to a debate about the nature of the two rival social systems, a debate in which we had nothing to fear and to which we were accustomed by debates with leftists within our own countries. Besides, Soviet "research" on their accusations against the West was so flimsy that in Ottawa and Bern it fell quite flat. A great weakness of the Soviets is that they believe their own propaganda about the West and get things amusingly wrong.

Meanwhile, I was determined even before arriving in Bern to maintain so quiet and level a tone that attention would be directed to the substance of what we said. Our charges were in fact so well documented and so damaging that they needed no tones of anger to heighten them. Faced with this tactic (it is also my normal style), neither the Soviets nor others could suggest that our two delegations were merely shouting at one another; on our part, there was no shouting at all. From my experience on the United Nations Human Rights Commission in Geneva, I knew that it was Soviet practice to shout, to bluster, and to try to intimidate. Answered with gentleness, such tactics easily backfired. So they did in Bern.

We learned later that, after a while, the Soviet delegation had had to throw away the blustery speeches that had already been pre-prepared for them in Moscow. Indeed, the head of the Soviet delegation flew back to Moscow after the second week. On his return, his own tone was much milder. He left the uglier replies to subordinates, who gloried in the old-style tactics. They did well what they were expected to do (I used to tell them). I especially enjoyed teasing Victor Shikalov, who had been a Soviet specialist on Helsinki since the beginning, building a career on his encyclopedic knowledge of the minutiae and arcana of precedents and events. "Victor," I told him more than once, "you deserve the Lenin medal for that performance this morning. They'll be proud of you in Moscow." On such occasions, Victor usually tried hard to maintain the appropriate Leninist seriousness and to repeat his outrage at the perfidies of the United States: but then he usually couldn't help returning smile for smile. He did seem to believe the propaganda he had heard all his life.

At the piano, Victor played Mozart, Beethoven, and other masters beautifully; he had started life with an ambition to be a concert pianist. He served his country well in the roles he was assigned: usually, to be the harshest denouncer of the West and the most thick-seated and stubborn Leninist negotiator. To tease him was delicious, most of all when he tried hardest not to break into a smile.

9
A New Beginning for Divided Spouses
APRIL 22, 1986

MR. CHAIRMAN: Let me begin by thanking my fellow delegates for the good spirit shown in our work so far. We are here, in the name of ordinary people everywhere, to review "developments in human contacts" since Madrid. It is easy for each nation to see ways in which other countries fall short of commitments we all made together, in one another's presence, and in the presence of ordinary people everywhere. This morning the distinguished delegate of the Soviet Union urged every nation here to see its own faults. Alas, he did not show us how. He did not practice what he preached. We hope that later on he will.

Today I would like to cover three points: first, an area in which the United States is reviewing its own conduct in the light of new realities since Madrid; second, a welcoming note for certain improvements in Eastern Europe since Helsinki; third, a proposal to make the Bern meeting a landmark for separated spouses.

By way of introduction, however, permit me to note a question of scale and degree. First, as all the world openly experiences, human contacts flow most freely among the free people of the free nations. Second, human contacts flow less freely within the nations held by the Communist Party: although not so freely as in the free world, better than ten years ago. Last of all come movements *from* the free world *into* the Communist world, and *from* the latter *out*. Here is the real barrier. Here is our real subject. This is expressed in the metaphor "Iron Curtain," in the Great Wall through the center of Europe, and in the "problem" of human contacts. At Helsinki and Madrid, all our governments committed themselves to lowering the barriers separating East from West. In meeting that task, the United States wants to do its share.

U.S. Visa and Immigration Screening

Criticism best begins at home. In the United States, criticizing government is a favorite habit of our citizens. Thus, Thomas Jefferson warned his contemporaries that the American commitment to "liberty and justice for all" would require a constant set of "revolutions." There is never enough liberty. There is never enough justice. Progress must be incessant. Every generation must attempt a new beginning. Since Jefferson estimated that the average generation lasts eighteen and a third years, he thought America should have a "revolution" every eighteen and a third years. That is the secret to our nation's dynamism and to our fascination with "new beginnings."

In the field of human contacts, concerning both immigrant and nonimmigrant visas, our nation faces an unprecedented volume of daily decisions. Our delegation listened with care to reforms on our part suggested here by others.

On this planet, liberty is more scarce than oil. Therefore, millions of persons constantly seek out the free nations. Of these, perhaps as many come to our country as to all other nations combined. Steadily, more than 500,000 legal immigrants settle in the United States each year, along with another 70,000 refugees. This comes to about 6 million new immigrants each decade. It is as if we added a new population the size of Switzerland every ten years. It means that 2,400 immigration visas must be processed every single working day of every year.

Still, this number does not include the millions of foreign citizens living and working in the United States who stream through our borders *without documents*. The cumulative number of these undocumented ones is estimated to be 12 million. Trying to control this flow has led to many perplexities. For example, we now require a valid visa for all visitors (except Canadians). This screening mechanism imposes an inconvenience, especially on those whose own countries do not require U.S. citizens to have visas. Again, current visa law contains provisions barring a very small number of visitors on grounds of activism in certain ideological causes. To many in the United States, even this small number of exclusions seems contrary to the openness we cherish. Fresh debate upon this question in the government, in Congress, and among the public is under way.

Just the same, in 1985 alone (a typical year), more than 6 million citizens from around the world entered the United States on nonimmigrant visas as tourists, students, visitors, and the like. For them, 24,000 nonimmigrant visas (on average) were issued every working day. By continuing to be a nation of immigrants, the United States is three ways blessed: in the newcomers, we see ourselves; they tie us to the whole human race; they enlarge our spirits. We welcome them, as we welcome, too, those who come for shorter periods.

Nonetheless, in the process of issuing more than 24,000 visas of one kind or another every working day, we know that we generate snafus, make mistakes, cause some delays, and need constantly to review our methods of operation and the changing patterns of global mobility. There are many debates in America today about several aspects of our visa policies. No one hesitates to criticize our government; to do so is our way of life. We want to do things better; in our view, improvement is always necessary.

Improved Contacts with Eastern Europe

Second, the people of the United States can hardly help welcoming improvements regarding human contacts in several Eastern European countries. That there are different social systems and different ideologies is no excuse for the diminishment of human contacts. As the distinguished representative of Austria pointed out last week, "Even among countries with different social systems, problems concerning human contacts need not arise." The borders between Austria and two of its Eastern neighbors, in this respect, are now remarkably open. We welcome that. We praise the countries involved. Again, although Poland's issuance of passports is sometimes arbitrary, it is undeniable that Poles are more free to travel abroad and to emigrate than they were four years ago. We welcome that. It is only honest to praise real progress engendered by the Helsinki Final Act.

Here I do not want to be misunderstood. The ordinary people of Eastern Europe are far from being as free as they have every right to be. In these matters, theories of moral equivalence are intellectually empty. For Communist nations, human contacts based upon individual rights and individual choice present profound difficulties. When planners plan human contacts, ordinary human will, unpredictable and uncontainable, is an annoyance which they can hardly help wanting to reduce, steer away, or prevent. Nonetheless, it is admirable that some states, although led by elites of the Communist party, are trying to incorporate the Helsinki notions of individual choice into their practices. This is a step forward for millions of ordinary people, whose experience cries aloud for it.

Divided Spouses

The third point I want to raise concerns one small category of human contacts cases: divided spouses. By this is meant, in the first instance, the marriage of two citizens from two different states in which, for some reason or another, one of the two spouses is prevented by state authorities from leaving that country. According to the Final Act, all such couples should be able to join each other in timely and permanent fashion, as those individuals choose.

Many of those who participate in human contacts under several of the subheadings of the Final Act—in sports events, as students, as tourists, in cultural exchanges, in travel for personal or professional reasons—are young. From time to time, they meet other young people in their host country. They fall in love; they marry. What could be more natural? What could better exemplify "mutual understanding and concord" across state frontiers?

Consider the two largest populations represented in this room, the Union of Soviet Socialist Republics and the United States of America. When U.S. citizens meet Soviet citizens, they often, quite spontaneously, like one another. When young persons from our two countries meet, they sometimes fall in love and marry. My delegation—and, I am sure, the Soviet delegation—wishes to go on record in favor of love and romance. I believe all delegations here will join us. Love, both faithful and romantic, is the great story of Western civilization, whose bewitchments no one better described than the great Swiss writer, Denis de Rougemont, in *Love in the Western World*.

Between the USSR and the United States, there are, at the present time, twenty-one cases of separated spouses. Since ours are nations of 270 million and 235 million citizens respectively, surely we can find a constructive way to bring such persons together swiftly, routinely, and in a positive spirit. We know this can be done, because it was recently done. At the time of the Geneva summit, eleven such couples were allowed to reunite. Their cases were, in all crucial respects, like the twenty-one remaining.

I hasten to point out that approximately one hundred marriages occur every year in the Soviet Union between American and Soviet citizens. The Soviet Union solves most of these cases at the first or second official request. We applaud this compliance with the Final Act. We were also glad to see the relatively sudden solution of eleven of the longstanding cases on the occasion of the Geneva summit.

The heartbreaking aspect of the remaining cases has three facets. First, the reasons given for denial by Soviet officials often vary and contradict each other. Second, the reasons given seem no different in principle from those of the cases solved on the occasion of the Geneva summit. Third, the real reason seems to be, not the ones expressed, but reasons of state.

No wonder, then, that the divided spouses are made to feel like pawns. They are sometimes told—we have heard the same words in this very room—that on such cases as theirs there will be no action until the international political situation improves. This means that individual rights in the Soviet Union are not unalienable. It means that individuals are regarded as instruments of the state. It means that the real reason for not moving on these cases is the priority of the state over individual rights. It means that the Helsinki Final Act is not permitted to function for individual Soviet citizens, but only for the Soviet state.

Mr. Chairman, we have been told that the Soviet Union does not regard the individual rights inherent in the Helsinki vision of human contacts as ends in themselves, only as means. The Soviet Union does not regard individual rights as "above" other matters, we have been told, but as items to be traded, like commodities, for other coin. For the citizens of free nations, this notion is both unacceptable and abhorrent to what they mean by "human." Individuals are not ants in an anthill, sheep in a herd, bees in a beehive. They are self-directing centers of insight and choice.

If current Soviet authorities really do regard the human being as an instrument of policy, a pawn upon the chessborad, a means rather than an end itself, they are underestimating the historical genius, the courage, and the conscience of great peoples we have all learned to love and admire.

Mr. Chairman, my delegation believes that a new moment may be at hand in the Soviet Union, in which human beings will come at last to be treated as ends, not as means. Human beings, so many Russian artists have taught us down the centuries, are the most valuable and precious beings in the universe. They are such because of the burning conscience within them, which the state cannot take away from them, whether under the czar or in the gulag. For that reason, we believe that Soviet authorities, under fresh leadership, will take a fresh approach to human beings, and first of all to these few cases of love divided—the twenty-one separated spouses.

At Geneva, for eleven happy couples, such a solution meant mercy, beyond the mere letter of the law. At Geneva, it meant generosity, beyond a narrow sense of the "interests of the state." To bring the remaining twenty-one couples together will also require statesmanship. It will require respect for the profound and unpredictable paths of love between man and woman. Tolstoy would have understood this, as would all the great writers and poets of our mutual humanistic and literary traditions. There are times when politics and ideology must yield to love. Humane values are deeper than politics and ideology; they are, in fact, their sole justification.

Some issues before this Experts' Meeting are difficult and involve large numbers. These cases of separated spouses involve small numbers.

41

In the second instance, I must also point out that in three of the pairs of divided spouses, both spouses were originally citizens of one country, but one has become a citizen of another, and it is in the latter that both have chosen to be reunited. The Final Act calls for favorable action in such cases, too. One of these couples, Anatoly and Galina Michelson, have now been held apart for thirty years. When states are powerful, international in their reach and scope, secure and mature, such states acquire new reasons for showing a positive spirit in such cases as well.

Bern might well mark a new beginning in at least this one type of case, of such numerical simplicity. Therefore, Mr. Chairman, can we not recommend that all the governments signatory to the Helsinki Final Act and the Madrid Concluding Document celebrate the Bern meeting by resolving the relatively few cases on the representation lists of all of us? Can we not wipe the slate clean? Let these few painfully separated men and women come at last together; let there be peace in this small number of human couples, as a symbol of the wider peace we all seek. Let there come from Bern a harbinger for all the world to see and to admire.

This would be but a modest gesture, Mr. Chairman. My delegation recommends it to the consideration of all the delegates gathered here in Bern. This spring in Bern, we are making a new beginning. Here all of us are pledging that our nations will do better in compliance with the Helsinki Final Act. What would constitute a better starting place? The number of cases is small, and love between married persons touches human hearts everywhere. My delegation would welcome, and fully praise, all steps made in this direction. A small gesture, we would regard it as quite significant: wiping the slate clean, for mercy's sake, in the name of a new beginning in the field of human contacts.

THE WORLD BEYOND BERN: CHERNOBYL

On Monday, April 28, Sweden announced that a cloud of radiation from the Soviet Union was blowing over Scandinavia and demanded an explanation. Only then did the USSR admit that a nuclear power plant in the Ukraine had been "damaged." The Chernobyl nuclear plant was located only sixty miles north of Kiev and its 2.3 million residents. The accident, which may have occurred as early as April 24, had been shrouded in secrecy, and at first the Soviets refused most offers of assistance.

Analyzing the radioactive fallout, western experts speculated that the reactor's core had experienced a partial meltdown. Official Soviet sources released few details of the disaster, and persons attempting to contact relatives in the area often found telephone service interrupted. By Tuesday, April 29, American spy satellites revealed that the reactor's graphite core was still burning; the resulting radiation and heat made it nearly impossible to approach the reactor and put out the flames. West German scientists estimated that up to 10,000 persons living within 300 miles of Chernobyl might die of lung cancer within ten years as a result of the disaster.

After declining to accept the assistance of experts from the International Atomic Energy Agency, the United States, Great Britain, Canada, and other nations, Moscow finally did allow Dr. Robert Gale, an American expert on bone marrow transplants, to come to Moscow on Thursday, May 1. Poland, 260 miles east of Chernobyl, restricted the sale of milk and vegetables contaminated by the fallout and required children to take iodine to help prevent thyroid cancer. All over central Europe, radio and television warned citizens to be careful of certain foods. The scare was real enough, and radiation levels were carefully monitored.

One does not use a national catastrophe as an occasion for scoring political points. The lack of information from the USSR—after our long debate on openness at the beginning of the conference—was acutely embarrassing to the Soviet delegation. Most western delegates, if they said anything at all, expressed sympathy for the victims.

When the story of Chernobyl first broke, I was in the offices of Radio Free Europe/Radio Liberty in Munich for the annual meeting of its governing board, the Board for International Broadcasting, and had learned at first hand how difficult it was to get accurate information. RFE/RL were extremely scrupulous in waiting for securely verified information. They refused to broadcast rumors or single-source stories (that were then appearing elsewhere in the western press) lacking strict verification. Often commended later for this scrupulosity—and for an accuracy that later information fully justified—RFE/RL gave me the best available information at the moment. I knew on my return to Vienna on Wednesday how fragile many stories then appearing in the press were. Listenership to RFE/RL shot up heavily during that period:

probably the single most reliable information available in Communist Europe. RFE/RL provided good examples of the two principles for which the West had argued in the opening sessions at Bern: openness and responsibility both to the public and to the truth.

Even when I received appeals from the U.S. Congress, expressing the concerns of their constituents for their families in Ukraine and Poland, I took pains to present these to the Soviet delegation with expressions of sympathy for widespread uncertainty and suffering. The lesson on the need for greater glasnost *spoke for itself.*

10
Family Reunification
April 24, 1986

Mr. Chairman: Before launching into the forward-looking points I want most to make, I must first complete a disagreeable task.

Correcting the Record

In the United States we play a game called horseshoes. A one-inch iron rod is set in the ground, surrounded by a pit filled with sand or sawdust. From an appropriate distance, the competitors toss iron horseshoes at the rod. Points are scored for ringing the horseshoe around the rod and even for coming close.

Yesterday the distinguished delegate from the Soviet Union tossed several iron horseshoes at the United States. We listened to every charge carefully. None rang the iron rod. All missed the pit completely. Most do not come under our mandate for this meeting, and so I would prefer to save us all time by answering them in written form, to be distributed to all delegations. Concerning those that *are* germane, though not quite accurately stated, allow me to make the following points.

The distinguished Soviet representative stated that thousands of people have been denied entry into the United States under the McCarren-Walter Law. In invoking in this context the name of Gabriel Garcia Marquez, a member of the World Peace Council, a Soviet front organization, he sought to insinuate that these people were refused on political grounds. In 1985, however, a typical year, only 330 people, many of them members of terrorist or Nazi organizations, were denied entry on such grounds. Gabriel Garcia Marquez has never been denied entry to the United States.

No American citizen can be prohibited from leaving the country, and no exit visa whatever is required. The sole exception applies to those for whom a court order has been specifically issued because a criminal warrant has been issued, or because the person is out on bail or on probation after conviction for a crime. The orange cards flag citizens for whom criminal warrants have been issued.

No U.S. representation list bears the names Victor or Mikhalina Balaban: not our list of divided spouses, not our list of divided families, not our list of dual nationals. In presenting the names of Anatoly and Galina Michelson, the United States is well aware both of the circumstances mentioned by the distinguished delegate and also of the fact that in at least two similar cases, the USSR has, after a time, acted in a humane spirit. The Michelsons have now been separated since 1956. Thirty years!

Praise for the Soviet Union

Right off the top, Mr. Chairman, allow me to praise the Soviet Union before criticizing it. It has been suggested in this room that no one here praises the Soviet Union enough. Although such a task can be bottomless, our delegation considers that the need for moderate amounts of praise is normal. Although we save our highest admiration for those states that delight in accepting criticism, we do believe that those to whom praise is in some measure due ought to receive it in that measure. For every case handled routinely, according to international law, according to international commitments, and with respect for the decent opinion of humankind, the Soviet Union deserves praise. We are glad to praise it for compliance. We would be happy to praise it more.

Family Unity

Today, my subject is family unity—that is, family reunification. It is a sad but undeniable fact in such a broken world as ours that families, too, are sometimes broken. Family members leave the countries of their birth for a new land and a new life; they hope to send for their loved ones at a later date. This was how my grandfather came to a new land and millions upon millions of others in times earlier and later. In most countries, at most times, this hope of family reunification has been realized. But in some countries, at some times, hopes are often dashed. Some countries do not accord their citizens the basic right to leave their country; they accord them only the duty to stay. In these countries, all too often, family members who wish to leave to reunite with their close relatives, to live again as fathers and sons, sisters and brothers, are not permitted to do so. They are held against their will. Recognizing this problem, hoping to put an end to it, the founding fathers of CSCE made it obligatory to "deal in a positive and humanitarian spirit with applications of persons who wish to be reunited with members of their family."

Eleven years have passed since this obligation was mutually accepted. We have now gathered together at this meeting of experts on human contacts to assess the extent to which it has been honored. Since the late 1950s my country has maintained representation lists of divided families. These lists contain the names of family members who have been denied permission to leave their countries to reunite with loved ones in the United States. They are regularly presented to representatives of the countries concerned, usually at high-level meetings. Individual cases from these lists are also regularly presented bilaterally at the diplomatic working level.

We know that many countries represented here have maintained and presented similar lists. We know that eleven years after Helsinki, there has been some improvement in several countries, but many families, many ordinary people, still remain divided. Alas, lists must still be maintained. Alas, again, the countries to whom we present these lists are invariably the same. These are countries from which ordinary people do not have the right to leave; on them, it seems, is imposed a duty to stay.

One such country is the largest country represented here, the Union of Soviet Socialist Republics. In his opening address, the distinguished Soviet delegate told us that no one in his country had any reason to leave, since the Soviet Union guarantees employment, housing, medical care, and social security. This might be true, Mr. Chairman, if humans lived by bread alone. It might be true, if all shared rights and privileges equal to those of the *nomenklatura*. But even in material terms, it does seem a little disingenuous, when applied to a nation that exhibits so many painful social and economic problems, many of them admitted by Soviet leadership.

Nonetheless, Mr. Chairman, it would seem perfectly natural for a large majority of citizens of his country, or any other, to have no wish to leave it. Normally, ordinary people love their country. They leave their country with regret, and they retain forever a certain longing for it. In the regions of the heart, no place replaces "home." On the other hand, citizens who leave one country for another become important bonds of language, memory, and love between two peoples. They live out in advance harmony and mutual respect between two cultures. The United States and the USSR would benefit by many more such human bonds. We need such human links.

For this reason, the United States would like to see family re-unification links between our two countries become as normal and easy as ours are with other countries. That is why, long before Helsinki, the U.S. first presented a divided family representation list of the Soviet Union in 1959. We have done so subsequently on at least twenty-five separate occasions. On these lists are found only those family members who have been refused permission to emigrate from the Soviet Union twice or more.

At present, there are only 125 families on our list, representing more than 450 persons. These numbers are about average for the list over the years, as cases have slowly been resolved and new ones added. In a significant number of cases every year, Soviet authorities move at normal speed, and requests are duly granted. But the flow does seem to be controlled, for political reasons, as we have heard expressed in this room.

In the mid- and late 1970s, for example, many more first-time requests for family reunification were granted than denied. This was the time of the greatest liberalization in Soviet emigration policy. During the period 1975–1980, most of the families involved were from Soviet Armenia. Armenian family reunification reached a peak in 1980 when over 6,000 Soviet citizens were granted exit permission to emigrate to the United States.

The situation has changed dramatically since then. After 1980, the number of Soviets granted exit permission for family reunification has steadily declined. From more than 8,000 in 1980 and 1981 together, the number fell to 490 in 1982. The numbers for the next three years fell from 420 to 181 to 151. Incidentally, the distinguished delegate of the USSR told us yesterday that during the years 1980–1985, the USSR gave exit visas to 6,773 persons. Actually, the U.S. figures of cases actually processed by our Moscow embassy give the Soviets greater credit than that. Our embassy's count shows more than 9,000. But 8,000 of these were in 1980 and 1981, and since then only a trickle.

A somewhat different curve describes the resolution of cases on our representation list for divided families. During the mid-1970s, Soviet authorities resolved annually between 25 and 30 percent of cases. In the late 1970s this percentage shrank to 15 to 20 percent. Between 1981 and the eve of the Geneva summit the percentage plummeted to less than 5 percent per year. Recently, however, in the wake of the Geneva summit, this trend has been reversed. Since the eve of the summit, Soviet authorities have agreed to resolve 15 percent of all cases on our presummit divided family list.

Mr. Chairman, we have been told more than once that we must recognize a link between how the Soviets see détente and Soviet action on family reunification applications. The implication is that the Soviets deliberately use family reunification as an instrument of foreign policy. Let me observe only that the Helsinki Final Act says that "the participating states will deal in a positive and humanitarian spirit with applications of persons who wish to be reunited with members of their family." It does not say that the participating states will deal in a positive and humanitarian spirit with such applications, depending upon political considerations.

Mr. Chairman, there seems to be a difference of principle here. The Soviets hold—if I understand their position correctly—that all human contacts ought to be regarded as in a balance with détente: so much détente, so many family reunification cases; improve détente, improve the numbers of cases resolved. If that is the Soviet position, Mr. Chairman, the reasons I gave against it two days ago stand. In our view—and in the exact words of the Helsinki Final Act upon this point—the principle is quite different. The rights to family reunification are prior to questions of foreign policy. These rights inhere in persons. They are neither given nor taken away by states. States must act upon these rights "in a positive and humanitarian spirit"—*not* in a wavering, conditional, political spirit. This seems to be the plain meaning of the text.

Again, Mr. Chairman, there is a crucial difference between fundamental human rights, such as the right to emigrate, and the normal commercial or cultural activities of normal times. The first may never be abridged. The second do follow the rhythms of international life.

Perhaps, though, the distinguished delegate of the Soviet Union will deny that Soviet decisions in family reunification cases are taken on the basis of politics. Perhaps he will insist, rather, that Soviet decisions in such cases are made in strict accordance with Soviet law. We listened closely when he stated in his opening remarks to this meeting: (1) that Soviet laws prohibit Soviet citizens with certain kinds of security access from traveling abroad; (2) that Soviet regulations defining family relationships prohibit certain Soviet citizens from reuniting with family members abroad; and (3) (as he stated last Wednesday) that these laws and regulations violate no Helsinki commitment or other international instrument to which the Soviet Union is a signatory.

One difficulty my government has in accepting such explanations is the evidence of the cases on our own divided family list. Most of the families on our list have never been told the reasons for their refusals and why they are now being kept divided from their families in our country. It is difficult to determine why they have been refused, when no reason is given, not even the reasons mentioned above.

In thirteen instances where we do have evidence on the grounds for refusal, insufficiently close family ties were cited. In eight of these cases the relationship involved was that of a parent to an adult child; in the other five, that of a sister to a brother. Permit me two comments. First, over the years the Soviet Union has resolved many cases in these categories. It continues to do so to this day. Indeed, almost all family reunification cases fit into these two categories. Second, the Helsinki Final Act obliges the participating states "to deal in a positive and humanitarian spirit with applications of persons who wish to be reunited with members of their family." The people in these thirteen cases so wish.

In at least eight other instances, families have been refused on security grounds. In general, my government does not recognize as legitimate refusals based on such grounds. We believe that everyone has the right to leave his country if he wants to. But even if one allowed for refusal in certain extraordinary cases, what is the evidence in the eight cases mentioned on our list?

One man has worked as a ship designer in Leningrad. Although he designed only commercial ships and private boats and had no contact with the military, he was given a security clearance making it illegal for him to leave the country for five years after termination of his employment. His employment in fact ended in 1979, but he is still being refused exit permission on security grounds. Another man worked as an engineer with a low-level security clearance in a Kharkov factory that manufactured, among other things, a small part for the space industry. The engineer did not work in that section of the factory, however, and had no access to it. The terms of his security clearance were to expire three years after he left his employment. He left the employment in 1974, but he has yet to obtain exit permission. A female engineer at a ship-building plant held a low-level clearance and did not work in the classified area of the plant. She left this employment in 1975 and applied for exit permission in 1978. She was refused on security grounds, which she was told would expire in 1982. Nonetheless, 1982 came, 1982 went, and she still continues to be refused on security grounds.

These last two cases, and indeed four of our eight known refusals on security grounds, are particularly interesting in light of General Secretary Gorbachev's statement to the French press before his October visit to Paris. The general secretary affirmed that persons refused on security grounds for five to ten years are now being permitted to leave. But four of the eight known security refusals on our divided family list go back more than ten years.

Our alarm at this apparent Soviet disregard for the assurances provided by the general secretary is tempered somewhat by new evidence. The general secretary's statement to the French press may now be beginning to be reflected in actual Soviet behavior. We note that when the above-mentioned female engineer applied for exit permission in January of this year, she was not refused on security grounds. Instead, she was refused for having insufficiently close family ties to her mother and her brother in the United States. To her mother and her brother!

Mr. Chairman, the relatively few persons on our divided family list refused on so-called security grounds are not missile experts or intelligence agents. They are ordinary people, separated from their loved ones, with whom they wish to reunite. In the past, the Soviet government has allowed other ordinary people to leave who differ in no detectable respect from those now on our lists. Many of those previously allowed to leave had earlier been on our divided family list, but others had been given exit permission straightway. Knowing this, and knowing these persons are not threats to Soviet security, perhaps we may be forgiven for being puzzled about the true reasons governing these cases. The Soviet government would do much good in this respect if it were to make public its rules for refusing exit permission on security grounds. Perhaps then we might see signs of justice, where none appears now.

In three cases on our divided family list, we have a particular tragedy. These are families divided by artificial divorce. Three couples were told by the Soviet emigration authorities that one spouse could leave only if he or she divorced the other. Only, that is, if the family were broken apart. We understand that there are many similar cases of this kind not on our list, particularly in cases in which the families in question were applying to go to Israel. In many of these cases, Soviet emigration authorities assured the family that the remaining spouse would later be allowed to leave. To this day, the three families on our list (and many more besides) remain separated, husbands from wives, fathers from children. Perhaps they were naïve in believing what they were told; perhaps they were even intemperate in obeying what they were told. But we must remember the extreme conditions under which they acted. These are not evil couples who deserve punishment. They are ordinary couples, now most cruelly dealt with—separated, betrayed by authorities, alone.

In eleven instances, Mr. Chairman, families on our divided family list were told their applications had been refused because positive action was "inexpedient at this time" or due to the "poor state of bilateral relations." I will make no specific comment on these reasons, except to express profound moral disagreement with such a principle.

Mr. Chairman, in looking through all of the 125 cases on our divided family list, and all the various reasons given for refusal, we are struck more than anything by the ordinariness of the people involved. They have no secrets; they are not political. They are like many others who have left the Soviet Union. The only thing remarkable about them is the tragedy they suffer, through no fault of their own.

The Soviet Union is not the only state that places artificial barriers in the way of family reunification. We have encountered analogous problems, sometimes in greater, sometimes in lesser, degree with each of the countries of Eastern Europe. Today, for example, one of these countries now shows a truly humane spirit in the application of its laws. Virtually 100 percent of the cases raised at the working level are resolved within a short time. At the other extreme, one of the participating states makes clear by the timing of its resolution of cases that exit visas are tied to political considerations and not to the objective qualifications of the applicant. Still another Eastern European country, despite allowing the highest absolute levels of emigration for the purpose of family reunification, does so only after an average delay of two years for each application during which time applicants are stripped of their jobs, their social rights, and, frequently, their homes. Again, the profound sympathies of our government go out to the Turkish minority in Bulgaria, particularly those who seek family reunification in Turkey. By administrative fiat, the Bulgarian government has simply denied the powerful family bonds between Bulgaria and Turkey. On future occasions, we shall have more to say about the hundreds of families in Eastern Europe who are kept apart from their families in the United States, without credible justification. We have steady hopes, however, that this situation will improve.

Mr. Chairman, I do not want to end these remarks on a pessimistic note. And I am pleased to say that I do not have to. Since the Geneva summit, Soviet authorities have agreed to resolve 15 percent of the cases on our divided family list. This has been the largest number of promised resolutions in so short a period since the late 1970s. These commitments came in the wake of President Reagan's and General Secretary Gorbachev's joint statement at Geneva on "the importance of resolving humanitarian cases in the spirit of cooperation." My government welcomes the resolution of these and other individual cases. And we strongly welcome General Secretary Gorbachev's statement to the Soviet Party Congress on February 25, calling for "the solution in a humane and positive spirit of questions of the reunification of families."

Of course, much more remains to be done. Many more cases await resolution. But there are reasonable grounds for optimism. With good will on both sides, we look forward to a day when ordinary families are no longer victimized by the ebb and flow of political considerations. We look forward to the day when divided families and divided family lists are but a sad and distant memory, from crueler times. When that day comes, as come it must, our joint efforts here in Bern will have borne solid and lasting fruit.

11
Response to
Soviet Charges of April 23
April 24, 1986

1. *Charge:* The U.S. plenary statement of Tuesday, April 22, slandered the Soviet Union.

Facts: The U.S. speech criticized certain aspects of Soviet emigration policy as contrary to Soviet undertakings at Helsinki and Madrid. To criticize the Soviet Union is not to slander it. To prove slander, one must prove untruth. No one has been able to show even a glimmer of untruth in what I have said. Although the truth sometimes hurts, I did not intend to cause hurt.

2. *Charge:* The United States is guilty of mass murder in Libya.

Facts: The U.S. government deeply regrets any loss of civilian life in Libya as a result of the U.S. retaliatory raid. Every attempt was made to avoid the loss of innocent lives. This policy sharply contrasts with Soviet behavior in Afghanistan, where the indiscriminate killing of civilians has been Soviet policy since December 1979.

3. *Charge:* Defying billions of ordinary people, the United States set off another underground explosion on the same day as the U.S. plenary speech.

Facts: The Soviet proposal of a nuclear weapons testing moratorium was a typical Soviet progaganda ploy. The Soviet Union proposed the moratorium *after* completing its latest series of underground tests. The Soviet Union, as other nuclear powers, conducts such tests to ensure the reliability of its systems. In proposing the moratorium, it hoped to present us with the following dilemma. If we agree to the moratorium, the Soviet Union gains a unilateral military advantage, since we have not completed our series of tests, designed to ensure the reliability of our systems. If we do not agree, the Soviets can use that fact in the sort of propaganda campaign they are now waging.

4. *Charge:* The United States is conducting a policy of racial discrimi-

---

Text submitted to the delegates in writing rather than orally.

nation and genocide against American Indians, including forced sterilization of Indian women.

Facts: The story about mass sterilization of Indian women is spun out of the allegation by an American anti-abortion group that the Indian Health Service, a government agency, was performing *voluntary* sterilization operations. The anti-abortion group believed that government agencies, operating with taxpayers' funds, should not perform sterilizations for which there were no sound medical grounds. At any rate, the charge was investigated and found groundless. Not even a voluntary sterilization program existed. But that seems not to have stopped Soviet authorities from picking up the original false report, embellishing it, and using it in their anti-U.S. propaganda campaigns.

We readily concede that racial discrimination existed in the United States for a long time and that racial and ethnic antagonisms still exist. The economic and social effects of that history are visible today, despite the abolition of all forms of officially sanctioned discrimination based on ancestry. The fact that a majority of recent immigrants to the United States are nonwhites from non-European areas and that they have integrated into our society at a truly amazing speed is clear evidence of the strength of the well-recognized American acceptance of a variety of ethnic groups into our social and economic system.

5. *Charge: Time* magazine of May 6, 1985, states that in the past twenty years thousands of people have been denied entry into the United States under the McCarran-Walter Law. Among them are a Nobel Laureate, Gabriel Garcia Marquez, and many other world-renowned figures.

Facts: The McCarran-Walter Law referred to by the distinguished Soviet delegate is, in fact, nothing more than the U.S. Immigration and Nationality Act of 1952, as amended. This act, as amended, is the basic U.S. law on immigration and citizenship. This act includes criteria for eligibility for the granting of tourist and other nonimmigrant visas. In order to qualify for such visas, foreign applicants must satisfy a U.S. consular officer that they do not intend to immigrate to the United States. We do not give nonimmigrant visas to immigrants. Immigrants require immigrant visas. We do not have a copy of the *Time* magazine issue quoted by the distinguished Soviet representative, but we are certainly willing to admit that over 12,000 people worldwide have been refused tourist visas over the past twenty years.

Of course, in linking the figure of thousands of refusals to the refusal of a visa to Gabriel Garcia Marquez, the distinguished Soviet

55

representative is engaging in a typical piece of Soviet disin-genuousness. The implication of his statement is that thousands of persons like Marquez have been denied for political reasons over the past two decades. In truth, there are three provisions of the U.S. Immigration and Nationality Act providing for denial on political grounds. Let's look at the refusal figures for those provisions for 1985. Under Section 212(A)(27) of the act, 27 people were refused; under Section 212(A)(28), approximately 300 persons were denied entry. These consisted almost entirely of so-called trade union officials from Communist countries and members of the PLO, terrorist organiza-tions, and Nazi organizations. Under Section 212(A)(29) of the act, 10 persons were denied entry.

As for Gabriel Garcia Marquez, Mr. Marquez has never been re-fused admission to the United States. Since he is a member of the World Peace Council, however, a Communist front organization, he is required under Section 212(A)(28) to obtain a waiver to enter the United States. Under terms of the later McGovern Amendment these waivers must be granted to all but members of Communist trade unions, members of the PLO, and members of terrorist organizations. In 1985, 47,853 persons required waivers; as noted above, all but 300 were granted. Mr. Marquez has always been granted a waiver.

6. *Charge:* What other country could think of making up for the Olympic games—a most ancient form of human contacts—a pin that says "Kill a Russian"?

Facts: We are not aware of the appearance of any such pins at the 1984 Olympic games. The implication of this statement is not only that such pins appeared but that they were produced by the U.S. govern-ment. The Soviet Union well knows that this is false. Production of such artifacts in my country could only be the work of small groups of extremists who are condemned by the U.S. government and the overwhelming majority of the American people. Such a pin is abhor-rent to my delegation, to our government, and to a vast majority of the people of the United States.

7. *Charge:* The film *Rocky IV* depicts the Soviet Union in the image of a stupid idiot.

Facts: The film *Rocky IV* was not produced by the U.S. government but by private film producers, as is their right in a free society. The film *Rocky IV* and similar films do not reflect U.S. government at-titudes or policy. Those in our delegation who have seen that movie found that the two boxers portrayed seemed to be approximately equal in intelligence. I should point out that many films are produced in the United States every year by U.S. filmmakers that are, to put it mildly, extremely critical of various aspects of U.S. life.

8. *Charge:* We picked at random from our files several names from the list of twenty-one couples referred to in U.S. plenary. One is Mikhalina Balaban, wife of Nazi collaborator Victor Balaban.

Facts: The U.S. delegation has no information on Victor or Mikhalina Balaban, so we do not wish to prejudge their case, if there is such a case. But we do have a current edition of our official divided spouses list containing names of twenty-one separated spouses. No such name appears on that list, or on the other two official bilaterial lists of divided families and dual nationals maintained by the U.S. government. We would be happy to share these lists with the Soviet delegation at its request.

9. *Charge:* The United States may not know that Anatoly Michelson, husband of divided spouse Galina Goltzman, mentioned in the U.S. plenary, is a criminal and that is why his wife has been denied.

Facts: The U.S. government is well aware of the circumstances of Mr. Michelson's departure, that he violated the laws of the Soviet Union by seeking refugee status in Austria after legally departing from the Soviet Union. We are also aware of at least two other cases identical to Mr. Michelson's in which the family members in the Soviet Union were subsequently allowed to leave. We welcomed these decisions by the Soviet government and hope it will be motivated by similar humane considerations in the case of the Michelsons, who have been separated now for thirty years.

10. *Charge:* The United States distorts the facts on family reunification. Between 1980 and 1985 over 6,733 Soviet citizens left to be reunited with relatives in the United States.

Facts: Our own records indicate that for the period 1980–1985 as a whole this Soviet statistic is approximately correct. It is, however, extremely misleading. Our records indicate that over 8,000 Soviet citizens, mostly Armenians, emigrated to the United States in 1980–1981. In 1982, however, that figure dropped to 490, in 1983 to 420, in 1984 to 181, and in 1985 to 151. Thus, the period cited by the distinguished Soviet representative as indicative of Soviet responsiveness on family reunification is, rather, a period of precipitous decline in Soviet responsiveness. Only this year, as a result of Soviet resolution of cases in conjunction with the Geneva summit, have these numbers begun to increase once again.

11. *Charge:* State Department reports or the foreign affairs manual for 1985 contains a list of categories of persons who are not allowed to exit from the United States. It includes persons evading debts, taxes, and alimonies; persons wanted by the police, investigation agencies, and judicial authorities; persons involved in drug trafficking, forgery of passports, and other papers. The list also includes persons whose names have been put on mysterious "orange" cards.

Facts: My delegation does not know where the distinguished Soviet representative obtained his information. We would be curious to find out. Let me assure him, however, that there are no regulations prohibiting U.S. citizens from departing from the United States. We require no exit visas of our citizens. U.S. citizens serving prison sentences, of course, cannot leave the United States while serving their sentence. Presumably this is the case with all countries represented here. The only other circumstance in which a U.S. citizen can be prohibited from leaving the country is under a court order limiting the travel of a suspect released from detention on bail or on probation, or of a person who is a fugitive from justice. We suspect this is also the case with most, if not all, countries represented here.

The mysterious orange cards referred to by the Soviet delegate are passport lookout cards. They contain the names of U.S. citizens who are fugitives from justice. U.S. passport agencies in the United States have the right to withhold passport services from persons who are the subjects of outstanding criminal warrants in the United States. We assume that most, if not all, countries represented here have similar mechanisms for locating and attempting to limit the travel of fugitives from justice.

12
Increasing Human Contacts

by Ambassador Sol Polansky

APRIL 28, 1986

MR. CHAIRMAN: In the course of our deliberations to date, my delegation has referred to factors that influence how the United States administers the flow of visitors to our shores. We intend to expand on these remarks in the remaining part of the general discussion and in the subworking bodies. Some of the remarks we have made about the practices of others have elicited criticism, both direct and indirect, by some of the delegates here. It seems that some of those reactions have overshadowed our expression of satisfaction at recent progress made in human contacts by those same countries.

To my distinguished Soviet colleague, let me reiterate that we welcome the increase in resolution of divided spouse and family cases since the Geneva summit. We regard these resolutions as a positive step. For our part, we intend to do everything in our power to build a stable, constructive relationship with the Soviet Union. Resolution of bilateral cases on humanitarian grounds contributes directly to that end. That there remains a long way to go should not distract attention from the progress already made.

In this same vein, I wish to refer to other aspects of human contacts that also contribute to mutual confidence and understanding among nations, aspects that have largely been passed over during our deliberations. I am referring specifically to those parts of the Final Act and Concluding Document that call for the further development of contacts among young people and for the expansion of sports ties and other forms of human contact.

Such contacts were the subject of extensive discussions between my government and the Soviet government in the preparations for the Geneva summit. They resulted in an agreement on a number of bilateral exchange initiatives designed to further such contacts. Agreement in this area was announced in the joint statement issued at the conclusion of the meeting:

> The two leaders agreed on the utility of broadening exchanges and contacts including some of their new forms in a number of scientific, educational, medical, and sports fields

59

(inter alia, cooperation in the development of educational exchanges and software for elementary and secondary school instruction; measures to promote Russian language studies in the United States and English language studies in the USSR; the annual exchange of professors to conduct special courses in history, culture, and economics at the relevant departments of Soviet and American institutions of higher education; mutual allocation of scholarships for the best students in the natural sciences, technology, social sciences, and humanities for the period of an academic year; holding regular meets in various sports and increased television coverage of sports events). The two sides agreed to resume cooperation in combatting cancer diseases.

Specific programs to implement the various provisions of this agreement are now being developed. In addition to this agreement on exchange initiatives, my government and the Soviet Union also signed at Geneva a new cultural exchanges agreement. These agreements are genuine signs of the desire of both our governments to increase the level of human contacts between our two countries. We welcome these agreements, just as we welcome the increase in resolution of divided spouse and family cases in the wake of the Geneva summit.

In the weeks and months to come we hope to explore further avenues for agreement between our countries in the field of human contacts. We are particularly interested in greatly expanding contacts between our young people. Recently, Katarina Lycheva, a charming young Soviet girl, visited our country as an ambassador of good will. We would very much like to see visits of young people repeated thousands of times every year. At the same time, we have sought to expand our formal contacts with other Eastern European states, with most of whom we have existing exchange agreements. On the very day this meeting opened, we signed in Prague an agreement with Czechoslovakia on cultural and scientific exchange.

One final word on the government-to-government agreements I have just mentioned. We look on these as a necessary means of developing and expanding contacts when there seems to be no other reasonable choice, when governments think they know better than their citizens. Our strong preference, however, is not to leave such matters in the hands of bureaucrats; rather, such contacts should be left to the interested individuals and organizations who share and know best how to pursue mutual interests. Happily, this is the course being pursued between the United States and most CSCE participating states, including some countries of Eastern Europe. We hope it can become the pattern with all CSCE participating states.

During our own meeting, the Swiss Youth Federation sponsored a conference of European youth organizations. They have forwarded to us a variety of recommendations to improve conditions for youth exchange and youth tourism in our countries. These proposals deserve our serious study, particularly as they apply to improving the openness of existing exchange programs.

Mr. Chairman, just as my government is very much in favor of expanding human contacts between our people and the peoples of all CSCE participating states, we are also interested in reducing and eliminating existing barriers to human contacts. I hope what I am going to say next will not be taken amiss by my distinguished Soviet colleague. I intend it as an exploration of what we consider problem areas, and where we think an exchange of views can be beneficial. At the same time, let me hasten to add that some are areas where progress has recently been made, similar to the resolution of divided family and spouse cases.

Let me begin with family visits. Since 1970 the annual number of visits by Soviet citizens to their U.S. relatives has fluctuated between 1,000 and 2,000. The peak year, which was also the peak year for emigration from the Soviet Union, was 1979—that is, after the Final Act was signed—when 2,283 Soviet citizens were permitted to visit their relatives in my country. Since then, regrettably, yearly totals have fallen off by about a third. We noted with interest the distinguished Soviet representative's statement last Wednesday that seventy-six Soviet citizens had been granted permission for family visits during the first twenty days of April. This rate of 114 per month, however, is 34 percent lower than the rate of family visits approved in 1979 and 10 percent lower than the rate of approvals in 1985.

As in all the aspects of human contacts we are discussing here, the situation in the other Eastern European countries varies widely. Only two of the six states allow virtually unrestricted tourist or family travel to the United States. In other states, private travel to the United States is almost impossible except for elderly citizens. At least one participating state routinely denies exit visas to citizens who wish to visit relatives in the West who have been members of organizations not in favor with that government. Such action is often successful in intimidating individuals from joining such organizations and freely expressing their views, but not in improving the image of that participating state with the American public.

Since my government does not monitor the foreign travel of *our* citizens, we have no reliable estimate of the number of visits made by U.S. citizens to relatives in the Soviet Union. Soviet officials have stated privately, and we also believe, that over 50,000 Americans visited the Soviet Union in 1985. But we have no idea what percentage traveled for family visits. We do know, however, how difficult it can be for Americans to visit relatives in the Soviet Union. Stays with family members are strongly discouraged. Applicants are told it can take four months or more to process their applications. Soviet officials instead encourage them to sign up for Intourist tours, which permit a quick meeting with a relative, often under restrictive conditions.

The situation is worse still for the tens of thousands of former Jewish citizens of the Soviet Union who have settled in and become citizens of the United States. They are barred from visiting their relatives in their former homeland for reasons that our distinguished Canadian colleague has characterized as bizarre and inexplicable. If the distinguished Soviet representative has just responded to this point, I did not hear it from the translator and I look forward to receiving a copy of his text. If we are to improve the human contacts between our two countries in the spirit of Geneva, one easy and important way to do so is to preserve existing family and ethnic ties. Facilitating family visits in urgent humanitarian situations, such as illness or death, is particularly important. I hope we all can agree on that.

We are particularly concerned about the many barriers to meeting Soviet people that still seem to await our citizens upon arrival in the Soviet Union. It is true that Americans and other foreign visitors can tour the grounds of the Kremlin and enjoy the treasures of the Hermitage in Leningrad, for example. But Gorky and Sverdlovsk, and a host of other Soviet cities and the people who live there, are off limits to them. This is because the Soviet Union has unilaterally and officially closed 20 percent of its territory to foreigners. In practice the situation is even worse. Foreign tourists in the Soviet Union are required to use Intourist accommodations and approved foreign transportation routes. This results in the *de facto* closing of another 75 percent of Soviet territory. The sad fact is that only 5 percent of the Soviet Union is genuinely open to tourists. This is not a policy that lends itself to improved human contacts.

The climate for human contacts in the open 5 percent of the Soviet Union is also not the best. As our distinguished British colleague has noted, a Soviet decree of May 25, 1984, established fines of up to 1,200 rubles for Soviet citizens violating rules of stay for foreigners in the Soviet Union. The decree set fines of up to 50 rubles for providing foreigners with "housing or means of transportation or other services" in violation of unspecified "established regulations." Instead, foreigners are limited to Intourist hotels, many of which are closed to ordinary Soviet citizens. Foreigners can receive travel services only in these few cities that have an Intourist office. Foreigners are required to pay much higher room rates, in hard currency. When traveling by train, they are frequently compelled to travel first class, charged higher fees, and deliberately segregated by cabin or car from ordinary Soviet citizens. These kinds of policies and practices do not, in our view, lend themselves to increased human contacts.

Some other governments of Eastern Europe allow fairly unrestricted travel on their territories by foreign citizens. A notable exception is Bulgaria, which has arbitrarily closed off 20 percent of its territory to all foreigners.

At least two Eastern European governments have established regulations, in some cases unpublished, forbidding or inhibiting contact with foreign citizens. One such law requires *any* contact with foreign citizens to be reported promptly to the police. Clearly such regulations run counter to the professed wish to improve contacts between ordinary people. Other regulations, in at least three Eastern European states, make it impossible for citizens to extend an invitation to other than close relatives for any overnight visit. It is ironic that such laws exist in countries that argue most strongly for free contact among youth, since their effect is most deeply felt by young people traveling on a low budget.

Mr. Chairman, I have been speaking so far about face-to-face human contacts, primarily family visits and tourism, but for most people foreign travel is still an infrequent occurrence. To keep in regular touch with friends or relatives abroad, they rely on the telephone or, even more frequently, on the international post. When these means of human contact prove unreliable, the cost in human suffering can be great.

Every year the U.S. Postal Service sends some 900 million pieces of mail to every corner of the earth. Yet of all the 167 countries with which this exchange takes place, our postal service has major problems with one: the Soviet Union. I regret to say that these are not problems of mail innocently misdelivered or inadvertently lost or delayed, but of mail intercepted and confiscated by Soviet authorities. Letters and parcels are returned as undeliverable when, in fact, they are deliverable. Registered items are reported on advice-of-delivery forms as having been delivered when independent information indicates the contrary.

On many occasions, intercepted mail contains invitations from family members to Soviet relatives who wish to visit or emigrate to my country. On other occasions, they contain only news and greetings between families and friends. Over the past several years, the U.S. House of Representatives Committee on Post Office and Civil Service has documented more than 2,700 instances of Soviet postal abuse, involving mail sent from twenty-four different countries. The U.S. Postal Service has itself received many times this number of complaints in recent years. In fact, they report that over the past five years the Soviet Union is the only country that has been the subject of such complaints. Mr. Chairman, postal communications should be guaranteed freedom of transit in accordance with the Universal Postal Convention.

On August 1, 1984, Soviet authorities ended a thirty-year policy that had permitted foreign citizens to prepay customs duties on parcels sent to friends and relatives in the Soviet Union. Now such costs, amounting to 30 percent of the value of the gifts, must be borne by these friends and relatives themselves. Since most of these people have very modest incomes by Western standards, they cannot afford to pay the duties. A very real and tangible form of human contact has thus been lost to them.

In 1981 Soviet authorities ended direct dial service to all parts of the Soviet Union save Moscow. In 1982 direct dial service with Moscow was also ended. According to Soviet government authorities, these steps were necessary for "technical reasons." It was suggested that necessary adjustments would take until 1984. We are now one-third of the way through 1986 and, although some direct dial service has been provided to Western European businessmen, the system has not been restored to others who also have legitimate interests in maintaining personal or professional contacts of a very human character. Other Eastern European countries generally do not find technical barriers to direct dial service. Bulgaria is now installing this service, which we trust will lead to unimpeded, private contact between its citizens and those of other countries.

Mr. Chairman, I must confess that the Soviet measures I have mentioned appear to us as attempts to erect barriers to human contacts rather than to eliminate them. They appear to us as part of a pattern of behavior during the early 1980s to restrict human contacts between Soviet citizens and the rest of the outside world. They appear to us as movements away from compliance with the Helsinki Final Act and the Madrid Concluding Document.

The early 1980s have come and gone; it is now 1986. A new generation of leaders has come into its own in the Soviet Union. Our governments have begun to take steps to increase human contacts. These are positive developments. We seek to build upon them. I have been outlining areas where we think that improvements can be made with little effort. No doubt there are areas where the distinguished Soviet delegate thinks we, too, could do better, and he has mentioned some of these areas this afternoon. We hope we can work together toward that end. By increasing the human contacts between our peoples, we will help build the stable, constructive relationship we both profess to seek. And in so doing we will enhance security and cooperation among all the CSCE signatory states.

13
Regarding Visa Practices
APRIL 29, 1986

MR. CHAIRMAN: Last Friday, one distinguished delegate from a country of great beauty and long-standing civilization called for simplification of visa forms, a point with which we certainly agree. While he stressed all the questions his government did not ask, he did not mention one crucial aspect of his government's policy. Tourist visas for his country are routinely denied to former citizens of that state, particularly if the applicant has become active in émigré organizations not favored by that government. This policy does not seem to represent the soft winds of détente. It seems to represent a kind of curtain, possibly not of iron but a little difficult to get through just the same.

In fact, visitors to his country accustomed, say, to the open border beween Canada and the United States, will be stunned at the border of this good and beautiful land. This border is defined, quite visibly, quite clearly, by very heavy arms, barbed wire, watch towers, dogs, and tanks. I wish this were not true; I hope it will not be true for long. If to mention such things is to injure détente, how would one describe the actual, physical deployment of such things? We cannot allow CSCE to mean "Candid Speech Completely Excluded."

My government favors much, much better relations with all of Eastern Europe, based on candor, openness, family kinship, and joint economic creativity in helping every area of the world to eliminate poverty and to raise standards of living, all of us cooperating in the peaceful exchange of goods and services—that is, those humble activities that most occupy human beings, happily, when they are at peace.

I would like to reflect aloud on the comments made by the distinguished representative of Poland about the visa practices of "certain Western participating states." I found that most of these comments had a constructive side; most can be helpful both to the people of Poland and to the people of the United States, who share so many bonds of history, of heroism, and of kinship. He also made several complaints that may apply to U.S. visa policy. In reply, I would like to offer the following comments.

It is necessary to understand the nature of many Polish visits to the United States. In his first speech, the Polish representative noted that governments may sometimes restrict the travel of their citizens due to shortages of hard currency. But we cannot accept this as a reason to restrict travel. We understand the importance of hard currency to the Polish economy, for two reasons. First, Poland seeks to encourage foreign tourists to visit Poland, in order to gain hard currency receipts. Second, Polish tourism to the United States also provides a net gain in hard currency for Poland. This positive balance arises, first, because relatives of Polish citizens pay virtually all hard currency costs associated with the travel and visit of their relatives and, second, because thousands of Poles are actually working in the United States, even when they do not have authorization to be employed there, and they remit the hard currency of their earnings to Poland.

Indeed so many Poles seek to come to the United States on visitors' visas, while intending to seek employment, contrary to the declared purpose of their visit, that in 1985 our officials were obliged to refuse somewhat more than the figure of 7,660 visitors' visas cited by my distinguished Polish colleague. We are eager to issue tourist visas to genuine tourists. We issued more than 50,000 in Poland last year. We have also a mechanism by which workers can receive legal permission to work temporarily in the United States. But we cannot issue *tourist* visas to those whose primary interest is unauthorized *employment*. To distinguish between these two separate purposes, experience has obliged us to ask thirty-six questions on our visa application form. These questions are designed to clarify the true purpose of the applicant's visit. Filling out forms, like standing in lines, is always a burden. They are a burden for those who receive, as for those who apply.

Consular officers are only human, and they do make mistakes. Their judgments are fallible. We regret any instance in which someone who truly intended only to visit was refused a visa. Sometimes, however, our consular officers err in the other direction, and issue visas in good faith to those who turn out not really to be tourists. In those cases, if the immigration authority at the border or airport finds clear evidence that the Polish citizen misled the consular officer about the purpose of his visit, the Polish citizen may be denied entry, despite holding a valid visa. This has happened only rarely.

The distinguished representative of Poland raised many good questions, and we would be glad to discuss in detail how American procedures can be improved and to explain how and why our current regulations function as they do. There is only one line in his remarks that I found inappropriate—a reference to "police-type interrogation." Ordinary Poles know what police interrogation really is. They sometimes experience it when they try to approach American consular offices, never after they enter there. Among Poles, there is a huge demand to travel to the United States; almost every family in Poland—even the pope's—has relatives in the United States. There is a deep source of kinship and love between our two peoples. For this reason, our consular officers in Poland are heavily overworked. They conduct visa interviews courteously, but quickly. They approve 1,000 nonimmigrant visas a week. In almost every case, a tourist visa is issued the same day as the application. In this respect, I should add, the government of Poland acts almost as speedily, issuing entry visas usually within twenty-four to forty-eight hours.

In our case, it is true that members of the Polish Revolutionary workers party must wait an additional day or two for their visas because of a waiver provision in our law. This is virtually automatic, and, in emergency circumstances, even this delay can be avoided. Otherwise, party members are treated exactly like other applicants. No Polish citizen is refused a nonimmigrant visa simply because of party membership. The representative of Poland also mentioned employment discrimination against Polish immigrants in some countries, unless they give up their Polish citizenship. This accusation simply does not apply to the United States. In fact, some Polish citizens, those who fled martial law after December 1981, are in a privileged position regarding employment. They are by no means required to give up Polish citizenship.

U.S. immigration laws apply equally to citizens of all countries, without discrimination. Experience shows, however, that because of Poland's economic situation (temporary, we hope), a higher rate of Polish visitors to the United States seek and find employment, contrary to the conditions of their visa. In trying to apply the law equally, our consular officers have experienced a higher refusal rate for Polish citizens than for any other country in Eastern Europe. The reason seems to be Poland's economic situation; it is not American law, which is the same for all.

Our people have close links with the people of Poland, and we want to make our entry procedures as open and fair as possible. So we thank the distinguished representative of Poland for his criticisms and suggestions, and look forward to working with him for the benefit of both our peoples.

14
Toward an Open Soviet Union
MAY 1, 1986

MR. CHAIRMAN: The Soviet Union is a great nation among the world's nations. Its 270 million citizens occupy nearly a sixth of the world's surface. Its navy operates on virtually all seas; it is a great military power. The talents of its peoples have long been praised. Yet—and here is the puzzle, Mr. Chairman—why does such a great nation whose activities are international in scope remain so outspokenly insecure, hesitant, and fearful about human contacts?

The citizens of the United States have, cumulatively, millions upon millions of contacts with all peoples of Europe every year (and with all the people of the world, for that matter). But in no other nation are the human contacts of our own citizens so often interrupted, prohibited, limited, restrained, controlled, steered, and obstructed as they are, alas, with the citizens of the USSR. Mail is not delivered. Telephone service is interrupted. Soviet authorities discourage Soviet citizens from talking with tourists or offering them hospitality.

The irony of this situation is that the people of the United States typically *like* Russians, Ukrainians, Georgians, Armenians, Uzbeks, and all the other citizens of the USSR, when they are allowed to meet them. The various peoples of the Soviet Union are warm-hearted, passionate, often excited about ideas, deeply moved by high art, full of sentiment. People to people, our peoples get along splendidly. And why not? So many Americans spring from similar stock; so many profoundly cherish the great novels, plays, poetry, and music of Russian and the other cultures of the USSR. When the great maestro Vladimir Horowitz played recently in Moscow, television showed tears streaming down many faces in the audience and would have shown similar emotion upon the faces of many Americans, too.

So it is ironic. Our peoples have genuine affection for one another. In moments of joy, such as the Horowitz recital, and in moments of tragedy mutually shared, as in the heart-stopping tragedy and painful suffering of the past few days [at Chernobyl], our peoples are as one.

And yet communications from the Soviet side are so thoroughly controlled, steered, and often distorted either by total silence or by horribly falsified propaganda about other peoples and other nations that no one can help noting an unmistakable fearfulness about human contacts exhibited by the Soviet state. Why is the regime of such a great nation so afraid of human contacts? Why? That is the question behind every intervention during these past three weeks. Why?

The reason cannot be ideology: (1) Marxist thought does not require the total control exercised until now by the Soviet regime; (2) other Marxist nations do differently; and (3) many Marxist thinkers propose much more open methods.

If the reason for the closed society cannot be ideology alone, neither can it be attributed to the fact that the Soviet social system is "different" from all others. For to assert that is to beg the question. *Why* is it different? What is the *reason* for such systematic control over human contacts as the Soviet Union practices, and concerning which every delegation in this room has considerable experience?

A great world power, one of the greatest military powers the world has ever known, has the right to be secure, unafraid, relaxed, and open. According to the Helsinki Final Act, it even has the duty to be so. And in the world of fact and ordinary realism, it has the full capacity of being so.

The Soviet state could remain a Marxist state and still be far more open than it is—open in its postal service, open in its telephone and telegraphic service, open in radio and television and every form of reading material, open in permitting visitors to travel as freely as they do in Switzerland and other nations, and open in allowing its own citizens to travel, to visit, and to emigrate, as they like, when they like.

The Soviet Union is powerful enough to be an open society. Why, then, is it not so? The peoples of the Soviet Union are attractive. The nation has to its credit immense accomplishments. All the world would like to know its citizens better, and to have its citizens know better all the great, buzzing, and vital world around them. Why not? Why not an open, large-hearted, free, and amicable Soviet Union?

Nothing in the ideology of Marxism prevents this. Nothing in the vast power of the Soviet Union requires otherwise. Logic, reason, experience, sentiment, the ideas of civilized people everywhere, the basic founding ideas of European culture—and the Helsinki Final Act, Madrid, and this very good dialogue we have been having in Bern—all these invite the governing bodies of the USSR to try a new path. All the world would applaud new decisions taken in this new direction.

These are the reasons *for* greater openness to human contacts. But there are also arguments *against* the closed society: (1) the closed society deprives its people of the stimulation of diversity, opposition, and unconventional ways of looking at reality; (2) any one culture is only one culture, but human creativity is fertilized by inputs from many cultures (and especially by the most contrary and opposite), for the human mind works by the clash of opposites; (3) the closed society leads to a decline of standards, from want of true intellectual challenge; (4) in a closed society, the roots of genuine culture—a true sensitivity to differences and to nuance—are slowly covered over by bureaucratic sludge; and (5) even the mode of controversy declines, since true argument is not permitted and true differences are not freely faced.

In sum, the closed society deprives its thinking citizens of intellectual air. They miss, they truly miss, the necessary contact of the human spirit with contrary ideas and opposing images and unaccustomed controversies. Surprise is the law of life. Surprise is the stimulus of the mind. The question for Soviet society, then, comes down to this: can it compete in a world open to surprise, to choice, to individual will? My own answer is, its people are worthy of the highest confidence, and they would benefit enormously therefrom.

Indeed, nothing would do more to build a new spirit of worldwide confidence, a new humanitarian outlook, a new sense of a common humanity, than new policies of openness by the Soviet regime. Allow the peoples of the USSR to be seen and known and conversed with, as they are—an attractive and talented people. Allow them to know all the rest of us, as we are, in our strengths and in our weaknesses. All of us are only human beings: only that. But nothing less. This is the cry of Europe; this is the heritage of Europe: out of many, one. In diversity, a common humanity.

Europe has two branches, from one same set of roots. East and West are not antithetical; the two branches belong together. They should be open to each other. They should strengthen each other. They should enrich each other. Being closed, one to the other, violates our profoundest vocation, and wounds our duty to each other. The task of the younger generation of Europeans everywhere (including those who are children of Europe, in Canada and the United States) is to make Europe one—an open Europe, a Europe of respect and affection, one for the other, each for all, all for each.

Freedom of Movement

The key to human contacts is the freedom of human beings to *choose* which human contacts they desire. In this planetary age of swift and cheap transportation, the whole world is open to such choice. The nub of human contacts, their living kernel, is the right of every human individual to travel and to set up a small universe of human

71

contacts wherever such an individual wills. One's own human contacts are a crucial realm of choice. To an unprecedented degree, modern men and women choose the company they keep.

Thus, the central characteristic of human contacts in our time is free movement from place to place, whether temporary or permanent or, indeed, circular and changing. Free movement no doubt has costs. Everything does. It introduces risk. That is precisely what is most human about it. As has been said: "Nothing ventured, nothing gained." Free movement makes burdens for bureaucrats, for social welfare agencies, for keepers of records. It also means the temporary shifting of human resources from one part of the world to another. When openness to movement obtains in all directions, however, human flows tend to change, double back, and circulate—to the universal enrichment of the entire human family.

The first step in such openness is free emigration. Emigrating individuals, and emigrating families, tie bonds of memory and understanding, of knowledge and instinct and love, between the peoples to whom they immigrate and from whom they emigrate.

That is why the world was encouraged during the 1970s, when several hundred thousand from among three of the Soviet peoples, in particular, began to forge new links between the peoples of the USSR and the peoples of Western nations. I refer to the rather massive migrations during those brief years—years too brief—of ethnic Germans, Armenians, and Jews from the Soviet Union.

Almost two centuries ago, Catherine the Great and Alexander I invited German settlers to Russia, where 2 million ethnic Germans still live. Dispossessed during World War II, incarcerated and confined for ten long years after the war, these German citizens of the USSR were finally allowed to settle in Western Siberia and Central Asiatic Russia. Their diligent labor in agriculture and industry has won them new respect and acclaim. They suffer, however, from great pressures upon their historic culture, religions, and language. When emigration became possible to them during the 1970s, 105,000 of these ethnic Germans returned to West Germany.[1]

Something similar happened among the 4 million Soviet Armenians, who have with great effort built up one of the most prosperous of the Soviet republics. After World War II, Soviet authorities invited Armenians abroad to return to their homeland; and some 250,000 gratefully did, to build a new Armenia. During the 1970s, Soviet authorities also allowed emigration from ancestral Armenia, and some 52,000 Armenians chose to leave—all this despite the prosperity they helped to build.

The third major people of the Soviet Union permitted somewhat free emigration during the 1970s was the community of Jews, up to 3 million strong, dispersed mainly in the three great Slavic republics—Ukrainian, Belorussian, and Russian—and, for the most part, in the great cities of Kiev, Minsk, Leningrad, and Moscow.[2] This is the third largest Jewish community in the world.

Among all the cultures of the world, perhaps few place as much emphasis upon the life of the mind and the life of the arts as Jewish culture does, from early family life through adulthood. This is as true in the Soviet Union as elsewhere. Figures from 1973 indicate that, while Jews in the USSR constituted only 0.7 percent of the Soviet people, they accounted for 6.1 percent of all scientific workers, 8.6 percent of all scientists, and 14 percent of all scientists with the rank of doctor (a post-Ph.D. degree equivalent). In the past thirteen years, these proportions have been shrunk by discriminatory factors, quotas, obstructions, and steadily growing campaigns of anti-Zionism and anti-Semitism.

During the 1970s, Soviet authorities allowed Soviet Jews—especially those from rural areas—to emigrate. Some 250,000 did so. Nonetheless, in 1981, the curtain dropped on emigration for all three peoples: ethnic Germans, Armenians, and Jews. Today, from all those groups, only a trickle of emigration continues. For example, in 1979, at the high point, 51,000 Jews emigrated. By 1984, only 896 were allowed to leave; in 1985, 1,140—just under 100 per month. So far in 1986, the numbers have dropped even lower. The numbers are equally sad for the Armenians and the Germans. Only 109 Armenians were allowed to leave during all of 1985 and only 406 Germans.

Soviet authorities occasionally explain away the closing of these spigots of free choice, a human right guaranteed in many international instruments and written in the human heart. They sometimes assert that Soviet law permits emigration, but few now want to apply for it. This explanation defies probabilities. Worse, it defies facts.

The German Red Cross has testified that as many as 150,000 ethnic Germans still want to emigrate; scholars estimate far higher numbers. Scholars of Soviet Armenia hold that 200,000 Armenians want to emigrate now. And it is a simple, cold fact that 370,000 Soviet Jews have already requested papers of invitation from abroad, as required by Soviet law for the first step in emigration proceedings. The cold fact is that 3,100 Jewish families, some 11,000 persons, are known to have applied for, and been refused, permission to emigrate. Yet, during the month just before we assembled in Bern, March 1986, there was registered one of the lowest totals of Jewish emigration ever. Only 47 persons were allowed to leave.

I regret to say that the horror the refuseniks suffer is barely suggested in that number: 11,000 persons. Many of the refuseniks have been fired from their jobs and forced to take menial work. University professors and physicians now labor as janitors and street sweepers. Some, unable to find employment, are now, ironically, subject to charges of "parasitism." Children are barred from good schools and universities. Many refuseniks are vilified, often by name, in the Soviet media. During the past two years, years (many of us thought) of hope, numerous newspaper articles and several television programs have singled out refuseniks as "Zionist subversives."

The more active refuseniks, who teach Hebrew or speak out openly against the refusal of authorities to let them leave, are subject to particularly harsh sanctions. At least sixteen of them have been convicted since autumn 1984, several on crudely trumped-up criminal charges designed to discredit them. Many others have been threatened, their apartments searched, their phones disconnected. I am very sad to say, there have also been cruel physical beatings: Vladimir Lifshitz, Josef Berenshtein, and Yuli Edelshtein, for example. So heavy was his beating Berenshtein was almost blinded.

The life of the refuseniks requires immense courage. Simply to exercise a fundamental human right is, for them, an act of heroism. This courage has not been lacking; its beauty is breathtaking. Many refuseniks, 311 families to be precise, have been waiting to leave for more than ten years. They have been given the usual reasons: fully one-third of them, a hundred families, have been refused on security grounds. General Secretary Gorbachev has said publicly that such reasons now hold for at most ten years. The evidence that would support such welcome words has not yet appeared.

Still today 11,000 refuseniks have been made pariahs in the country of their birth. They should be allowed to follow their choice, to honor the good name of their country, and to become human links between the Soviet Union and their new lands of choice, helping to unite this broken world. That was the hope of Helsinki's Final Act.

And what of the 370,000 Jews who have received the necessary invitations to emigrate, but are afraid of becoming refuseniks? For external consumption, Soviet officials deny their very existence. They say that all who want to leave have already left, so no more problem. For internal consumption, though, a different story is told, closer to the truth. At a recent Znaniye Society lecture in Moscow, for example, an official Soviet expert on Soviet nationality policy estimated that between 10 and 15 percent of Soviet Jews now wish to emigrate. As his base, he used the 1979 Soviet census figure (showing a total Soviet Jewish population of 1.8 million). The Soviet Jews who wish to leave number, in his view, between 180,000 and 270,000. This falls short of the 370,000 known to have taken the first legal step. That percentage is closer to 20 percent. But this Soviet scholar's internal estimate is far larger than what his government claims externally.

To help make these numbers concrete, I have attached an annex to these remarks for distribution to every delegation and for the record, containing the names of a small fraction of those involved. This list helps us all to visualize the human persons behind the numbers. It helps us to imagine the new fields of human contacts they so persistently and bravely seek to enter.

Mr. Chairman, the obstruction to Soviet emigration is not a hurdle faced only by Armenians, Germans, and Jews. It is a universal problem in the Soviet Union, extending to every man, woman, and child in the country. We have focused on Armenians, Germans, and Jews only because they alone of the many peoples of the Soviet Union have been allowed to leave in significant numbers. Many Russians, Ukrainians, Balts, and others would leave if they could. We know the names of some who have tried and failed. But Russians, Ukrainians, Balts, and others know that members of their nationalities simply are not allowed to leave. For them there is no similar precedent; there is no similar hope. For many of them, the only method left is described by authorities as illegal: clandestinely, they simply flee. Many on trips abroad must leave "hostages" behind—a child, a spouse, a parent.

Consider the young Estonian official and his beautiful wife, a singer, who recently asked asylum in Sweden. The only way they could leave Estonia, sadly, was to leave behind their infant daughter. That infant, Kaisa Randpere, is now only two years old. Her grandmother, her guardian now, has been deprived of employment and threatened with confinement in an asylum for the insane. A great power could soften the crying of a two-year-old, allowing her now to join her parents, without any damage to its security, gaining honor for its open ways. A Europe without openness would be a hell; that is why Europeans so honor openness.

Openness: The European Imperative

In the course of our delegation's plenary statements, we have tried our best to give credit and to stress hope. We have tried hard not to be confrontational but to speak the truth as we see it fairly and clearly, in the context of much hope for better times to come. The Soviet Union has promised new directions. Here in Bern we strongly welcome every sign of spring.

In candor, we have suggested the enormity of the work remaining to be done, the boldness of promises yet to be fulfilled. As these promises become realities in fact—when the great nation of the Union of Soviet Socialist Republics opens itself to the world—a great new age of human confidence will have begun. That was the hope generated by the Helsinki Final Act. May it soon become fact.

Never more than now, Europe desires openness. The European vocation is openness. The European imperative is openness.

Notes

1. For recent studies of these emigrations, see the papers presented before the U.S. Commission on Security and Cooperation in Europe, April 22, 1986, the Congress of the United States: Sidney Heitman, "German and Armenian Emigration from the USSR"; William Korey, "Statement of William Korey on Jewish Emigration from the USSR"; and Felice D. Gaer, "The Right to Leave: East European Emigration Policies."

2. See also Allan Kagedan, "Gorbachev and the Jews," Commentary (May 1986), pp. 47–50; and Human Contacts, Reunion of Families and Soviet Jewry (Institute of Jewish Affairs: London, 1986); Kagedan uses the official Soviet figure (1979) of 1.8 million Jews.

Annex: Cases of Soviet Denial of Human Contacts in the Area of Family Reunification, Freedom to Choose One's Place of Residence

The following individuals have been denied permission to emigrate from the Soviet Union to various countries throughout the world. Since this is merely an illustrative list of the names of some of the people whose situations have become international cases, no significance should be attached to the presence or absence of any specific name on this list.

Refused over Ten Years on Security Grounds

BENJAMIN BOGOMOLNY: Benjamin Bogomolny first applied to emigrate with his parents in 1966. His parents and sisters were permitted to emigrate, but Benjamin was drafted into the army, where he served in a construction battalion. He reapplied on his own in 1972 but was refused because of his army service. All of his applications since that time have been refused on the same grounds. Over the years, he has been regularly harassed, his phone has been disconnected, his apartment ransacked, his books confiscated. His wife, Tanya, lost her job at the University of Moscow after she married Benjamin and it became clear that she wished to emigrate to Israel. Her immediate family emigrated in the 1970s, but she chose to wait with her husband. She now has cancer.

ALEXANDER LERNER: Professor Alexander Lerner is an internationally known authority in the field of cybernetics. After applying to emigrate to Israel in 1971, he was dismissed from his position as a director in an institute and professor and his visa refused on the grounds that "no decrees pertain to his situation." In 1976, the reason for refusal changed to "knowing state secrets." Despite numerous instances of harassment by Soviet authorities over the years, Lerner continues efforts to join his daughter in Israel.

NAUM MEIMAN AND INNA KITROSSKAYA-MEIMAN: A doctor of mathematics, Naum Meiman was a member of the Moscow Helsinki monitoring group. In 1974, he applied to emigrate to Israel but was refused on security grounds based on work he performed in the early 1950s. All his refusals since then have been based on the same grounds. Meiman's ailing wife, Inna Kitrosskaya-Meiman, first applied in 1979. They have been married since 1981. She has been refused permission to seek cancer treatment in the West, despite invitations from Sweden, France, the United States, and Israel. In September 1985, Mrs. Meiman applied to the director of Ovir to let her emigrate with her mother, brother, son, and two grandchildren, leaving her husband behind. On September 18, Mrs. Meiman was told that she could not leave with the other members of her family because she had been married to

Naum too long and her departure would constitute a security risk for the Soviet Union.

Refusals on Security Grounds—No Past Secret Work

LEV BLITSHTEIN: Lev Blitshtein and his family first applied to emigrate in August 1974. The Blitshteins were advised by Ovir to divorce so that his wife and two children could emigrate, which they did in 1976. Mr. Blitshtein has been repeatedly refused permission to rejoin his family, because of possible knowledge of Soviet meat production, although he has been told by the Ministry of Meat and Dairy Industry of the RSFSR that they have no claims against him since he never had access to secret documents.

Reason Given as "Poor State of Bilateral Relations"

VLADIMIR AND MARIA SLEPAK: Vladimir and Maria Slepak first applied to emigrate in 1970. A member of the Moscow Helsinki monitoring group and Jewish emigration activist, he was arrested, together with his wife, in June 1978, after they barricaded the doors to their apartment and displayed a banner on their balcony asking to join their son in Israel. Mr. Slepak was sentenced to five years internal exile, and Maria was given a three-year suspended sentence for "malicious hooliganism." Their two sons were permitted to emigrate, but the Slepaks have been repeatedly refused permission.

Family Ties Abroad Said Not to Be Close Enough

LEV ELBERT: Lev Elbert, his wife, and son, of Kiev, have been attempting to emigrate since August 1976. They have repeatedly been denied permission to join Mrs. Elbert's mother and brother in Israel on grounds of "secrecy" and later on grounds of "insufficient kinship."

Former Jewish Prisoners of Conscience Refused Exit Visas

IDA NUDEL: Ida Nudel has been attempting to emigrate to Israel since May 1971. She was sentenced in 1978 to four years of internal exile after displaying a banner reading "K.G.B., Give Me a Visa" in Moscow. After her return from exile, she was not permitted to reside in her home in Moscow; after months of searching for a city that would give her a residence permit, she settled in Bendery, Moldavia. She is known among other refuseniks as a "guardian angel" for her work on behalf of prisoners of conscience.

Other Former Jewish Prisoners of Conscience Denied Exit Permission

VIKTOR BRAILOVSKY: Moscow. First refused 1972. Released from prison 1984.

BORIS CHERNOBILSKY: Moscow. First refused 1976. Released 1982.

78

KIM FRIDMAN: Kiev. First refused 1971. Released 1982.

GRIGORY GEYSHIS: Leningrad. First refused 1978. Released 1982.

VLADIMIR KISLIK: Kiev. First refused 1974. Released 1984.

FELIKS KOCHUBIEVSKY: Novosibirsk. First refused 1978. Released 1985.

EVGENY LÈYN: Leningrad. First refused 1978. Released 1982.

OSIP LOKSHIN: Kishinev. First refused 1980. Released 1984.

MARK OCHERETYANSKY: Kiev. First refused 1979. Released 1984.

ALEKSANDR PANAREV: Sukhumi. First refused 1973. Released 1984.

ALEKSANDR PARITSKY: Kharkov. First refused 1977. Released 1984.

DMITRY SHCHIGLIK: Moscow. First refused 1973. Released 1981.

SIMON SHNIRMAN: First refused 1977. Released 1986.

VLADIMIR TSUKERMAN: Kishinev. First refused 1974. Released 1984.

Soviet Pentecostals

PAVEL AKHTEROV: A Pentecostal emigration activist, he was sentenced on December 28, 1981, to seven years of strict regimen camp plus five years internal exile for "anti-Soviet agitation and propaganda."

GALINA BARATS: This Pentecostal emigration activist was arrested in March 1983 and was later sentenced to six years of strict regimen camp plus three years of internal exile.

VASILY BARATS: A Pentecostal emigration activist, he was one of the founders of the Soviet Right to Emigrate Group in 1980. In September 1982, he was sentenced to five years of strict regimen camp and has had at least one heart attack.

VALENTINA GOLIKOVA: This member of the Freedom to Emigrate Committee was arrested in October 1984 and later sentenced to three years of ordinary regimen camp.

IVAN MALAMURA: A Pentecostal bishop from Tapa, Estonia, he was denied permission to join his daughter and son-in-law in Canada. Reportedly declared hunger strike "to the end," as of May 1, 1986, to protest denial of emigration request, loss of employment, harassment of his family by authorities.

FYODOR SIDENKO: A Pentecostal emigration activist, he was released from the Chernyakhovsk Special Psychiatric Hospital two days before the U.S.-Soviet Summit meeting. Arrested in October 1979 and charged with "anti-Soviet slander," Sidenko was subjected to intensive drug treatments in hospital.

Members of Other Soviet Nationality Groups Attempting to Emigrate

EDITA ABRUTIENE (Lithuanian): She was sentenced to a six-year term of imprisonment in July 1983 for her efforts to emigrate from Lithuania with her husband and young son. Her husband, Vitas Abrutis, had just returned from serving a political sentence in the camps when she was arrested.

NIKOLAI BARANOV (Russian): A worker from Leningrad, he served a five-year camp term on political charges for his emigration efforts. In November 1983, he was diagnosed as mentally unstable because he wanted to leave the USSR to accept an invitation to live in England. As of November 1985, he was being held in the Leningrad Special Psychiatric Hospital.

BALYS GAJAUSKAS (Lithuanian): He has spent over thirty-three of his sixty years in prison for Lithuanian national and human rights activities. He and his family wish to emigrate to join relatives in the United States.

EDUARD GUDAVA (Georgian): A Georgian Catholic, he has been attempting to emigrate for four years with his mother and brother, Tenghiz. In January 1986, Eduard was sentenced to a four-year prison term for "malicious hooliganism" for hanging a protest banner from the balcony of their apartment.

MIKHAIL KAZACHKOV (Russian): A Russian physicist, he was arrested in 1975 at the Leningrad Ovir when he tried to submit emigration documents. Accused of spying (he had visited the U.S. Consulate), he was sentenced to a fifteen-year camp term; in camp he received an additional three-and-a-half year term.

VARTAN KETENDZHYAN (Armenian): He was refused, along with his wife and children, permission to emigrate to join his brother and sisters in the United States. He has been rejected six times since May 1980.

IVAN MARTYNOV (Russian): A Russian literary scholar, he has been trying to emigrate to Israel since 1982. In January 1985 he was sentenced to eighteen months compulsory labor. Afterward, he was in a psychiatric hospital and subjected to forcible drug treatment for applying to emigrate.

ALEKSANDR MAKSIMOV (Ukrainian): When he became sixteen in 1975, he renounced his Soviet citizenship and applied to emigrate. He has served two labor camp sentences (1980–1981 and 1982–1984) for his emigration efforts. His mother Galina was sentenced to a three-year camp term in 1982 and reportedly was rearrested in camp.

IGOR OGURTSOV (Russian): He was sentenced in 1967 to fifteen years of imprisonment and five years of internal exile for engaging in religious activities and for founding the all-Russian Christian Social Union. The U.S. House of Representatives recently passed a resolution urging that Mr. Ogurtsov be released from internal exile and permitted to emigrate to the West without renouncing his views.

KAISA RANDPERE (Estonian): Two-and-a-half-year-old Kaisa has been separated from her Estonian parents since 1984, when they decided to remain in Sweden while visiting there. Kaisa is living with her grandmother, who has been harassed by Soviet authorities who have threatened to take the child away and put her in an orphanage. The Soviet government has rejected four applications submitted by Kaisa's parents for her emigration to Sweden.

JANIS ROZHKALNS (Latvian): A Latvian Baptist, he applied to emigrate in January 1983 together with nineteen other Latvians. Arrested in April 1983, Rozhkalns was sentenced in December to five years of strict regimen camp, plus three years of internal exile.

NIKOLAI SHABUROV (Russian): In 1982, he applied in his native Mariiskaya ASSR to come to the United States to study in a seminary. A few days later, he was arrested and committed to a psychiatric hospital.

ALEKSANDR SHATRAVKA (Russian): Originally placed in a psychiatric facility for trying to escape from the Soviet Union, he has frequently expressed the desire to emigrate. He is now in a labor camp for his activities as a member of the Soviet Independent Peace Movement.

YURI SHUKHEVICH (Ukrainian): He has spent over thirty-three of his fifty years in prison for alleged nationalist activities and is reportedly almost blind. He has relatives in Australia who are willing to accept him and his family and to support them.

ALGIRDAS STATKEVICIUS (Lithuanian): A physician and member of the Lithuanian Helsinki group, he is now incarcerated in a psychiatric facility for political prisoners. He wishes to emigrate and join his sister in the United States.

Other Soviet Emigration Cases

ROSALIYA BALANA: Refused permission to emigrate to Israel since 1980.

NATASHA BEKHMAN: Refused permission to emigrate to Israel since 1982.

ALBERT AND EDUARD BURSHTEIN: Refused permission to emigrate to Israel since 1980.

YULI AND TATIANA EDELSHTEIN: Refused permission to emigrate to Israel since 1978. Yuli is currently in prison.

LEV AND OLGA FABRICANT: Refused permission to emigrate to Israel since 1979.

IOSEF AND BELLA GLASER: Refused permission to emigrate to Israel since 1978.

CHERNA GOLDORT: Refused permission to emigrate to Israel since 1975.

ALEX JOFFE: Refused permission to emigrate to Israel since 1976.

ALEKSANDR KALMYKOV: Refused permission to emigrate to the United States.

SEMYON AND VERA KATZ: Refused permission to emigrate to Israel since 1979.

GENNADY AND NATASHA KHASSIN: Refused permission to emigrate to Israel since 1978.

ALEXANDER KHOLMYANSKY: Refused permission to emigrate to Israel since 1980 (currently in prison).

KARL KLESMAN: Refused permission to emigrate to Israel since 1980.

BORIS AND ELENA KLOTZ: Refused permission to emigrate to Israel since 1980.

BORIS KRIPOVAL: Refused permission to emigrate to Israel since 1981.

YELENA KRYLOVA: Refused permission to emigrate to the United States.

EVGENY AND IRINA LEIN: Refused permission to emigrate to Israel since 1978.

VALERY AND JANNA LERNER: Refused permission to emigrate to Israel since 1977.

VLADIMIR LIFSHITZ AND FAMILY: Refused permission to emigrate to Israel since 1981. (Vladimir is currently in prison.)

JOSEPH AND LEA PEKAR: Refused permission to emigrate to Israel since 1978.

VLADISLAV AND RIANNA ROYAK: Refused permission to emigrate to Israel since 1977.

LEV AND LEAH SHAPIRO: Refused permission to emigrate to Israel since 1977.

LEV SHEFER: Refused permission to emigrate to Israel since 1977.

MARK AND SVETLANA TERLITSKY: Refused permission to emigrate to the United States since 1976.

MIKHAIL TZIVIN: Refused permission to emigrate to Israel since 1981.

LEONID, LUDMILA, AND KIRA VOLVOLSKY: Refused permission to emigrate to Israel since 1974. (Leonid is currently in prison.)

IOSIF ZARETSKY: Refused permission to emigrate to Israel since 1981.

ZAKHAR AND TATIANA ZUNSHAIN: Refused permission to emigrate to Israel since 1981. (Zakhar is currently in prison.)

ALBERT AND EDUARD BURSHTEIN: Refused permission to emigrate to Israel since 1980.

15

The Right to Be Issued a Passport

MAY 6, 1986

MR. CHAIRMAN: I speak now in support of two proposals of which our delegation is a cosponsor. Each deals directly with ways of improving the lives of people and ways of protecting the credibility of the process in which all our nations are engaged. These are modest steps, which outside observers must find not only reasonable but virtually included in propositions already accepted at Helsinki and Madrid.

The first of these is BME 16, cosponsored by Italy, the Netherlands, and the United Kingdom. It establishes a time limit for the publication of laws, regulations, and criteria of judgment that affect travel and emigration. Its operative part calls upon the participating states to "publish within one year all laws, regulations and procedures—including criteria for refusal—governing decisions to permit their citizens to leave their country, on a permanent or temporary basis; and take steps to help make the laws that are in force accessible to all strata of the population of the country."

The reason for this clarification of existing commitments is as plain as the snow-covered Alps in the sunshine. To share the light of reason, laws must be brought from darkness into light. To be obeyed, laws must be known. Alas, in several participating states, citizens are not properly informed about what the law is, about the procedure for complying with it, and about the criteria of judgment employed to measure compliance. Laws so dark frustrate reason.

Several delegations, including my own, spoke on this matter earlier. The practical problem is serious. A prerequisite for the exercise of rights is to have knowledge of any laws and regulations that affect their exercise. The participating states clearly affirmed this point in principle 7 of the Final Act and reaffirmed it in the Madrid Concluding Document. Unfortunately, in several participating states, persons are often refused travel or emigration permission without any specific reason being cited for the refusal. Sometimes the number of an unpublished law or regulation is cited. Often, however, the person involved has no access to the text by which to determine the actual requirements of the law applied to their case. Left in darkness, such citizens have no informed grounds on which to appeal. Other persons are told only of "reasons of state" or unspecified grounds of "national security."

One example may be cited from the highest official authorities of one participating state. In 1982, these authorities provided a letter written to forty-four persons who had inquired about an appeal against the refusal of an exit visa. The response, sent by the highest legal authority of the participating state, affirmed in these exact words: "Emigration from [this state] is not legislated. It is directed and monitored by the Ministry of the Interior, *whose instructions are classified and unpublished.*"

Mr. Chairman: The proposal we have tabled refers only to laws and regulations affecting travel. But it is important to note that other human contacts are also affected by unpublished laws and regulations. For example, the law of one participating state, dated May 25, 1984, imposes fines against its citizens for certain types of contacts with foreign travelers "in violation of the established rules." This law does not mention what the "established rules" actually *are.* Thus, citizens have no way of determining what is actually allowed and what is not. Such ambiguity increases the possibility of a capricious enforcement of the rules. Citizens are placed in the position of taking a risk on any occasion when they have an "unauthorized," spontaneous contact with a foreign visitor. This practice chills human contacts. More sunshine would warm them.

Naturally, the simple publication of laws and regulations affecting travel will not, in itself, change repressive practices. Restrictive laws, whose texts are fully available to the public, will continue to diminish human contacts. Open publication will, however, provide applicants with specific information about the requirements of law. With such information open and available, they can then: (1) make better-informed decisions concerning whether to apply to travel; (2) develop an informed basis for appealing decisions already taken; and (3) obtain clear information for evaluating existing laws and regulations in the light of various international instruments. If the details of these laws and regulations are public, and if criteria for judgment are known to all, subjective error will be reduced.

By contrast, when laws and regulations affecting travel or emigration are *not* published, or if government authorities refuse to give specific reasons for decisions based upon them, even on appeal, then individuals are unprotected and vulnerable. Darkness is an enemy of human contacts. Openness clarifies the ground.

My delegation has also introduced proposal BME 14, cosponsored by Canada, France, and Greece. Its operative section calls upon states to "give special attention to and deal favorably with applications from their citizens or nationals who are also recognized as citizens or nationals by another state to leave in order to visit that state or to settle there."

This brief proposal deals with that very small number of persons who, either through birth or naturalization, are recognized as citizens by two states. Such persons, for example, are citizens of a participating state other than the one in which they are residing. The state in which they are resident claims them as citizens, but they wish to leave that state. There are, for example, twenty-one American citizens resident in another participating state who have not been permitted by its authorities to depart. There are a handful of U.S. citizens in the same situation in two other participating states.

I do not want to go into great detail about these cases, but it is necessary to provide some background. These twenty-one cases involve mostly persons whose parents were U.S. citizens who went to that other state in the 1920s or 1930s. They went either on contract to do jobs connected with the massive construction projects of that period or to return to the country of their birth out of a sense of new hopes following a revolution. Many of the children of such persons were born in the United States. Others, though born in the state where their parents took up residence, derive their U.S. citizenship through their parents.

It was certainly the right of those U.S. citizens to go to that state of their own free choice, though we do know that some later sought to leave and were prevented from doing so. In adulthood, many of their children have sought to leave to take up life in the United States, as their citizenship entitles them to do. This has been forbidden, in some cases after efforts stretching over nearly forty years. I must add that in many cases, the family involved never requested or sought citizenship in the state of residence. Many were simply informed in the late 1930s that they had been "granted" citizenship in that state, without their knowledge or application. Some have thus been caught in a citizenship they never claimed for themselves.

Mr. Chairman, the laws of many of our participating states do not recognize the concept of dual nationality. This is true also of the United States. Problems do not arise in most participating states in this regard, however, because persons are free to leave most nations simply by choosing to do so, in accordance with international law and the Universal Declaration of Human Rights. But a few participating states nonetheless insist that dual nationals must apply for exit permission solely on the grounds of family reunification. Unfortunately, many individuals on our list have no relatives (or no close relatives) in the United States. They find it difficult or impossible to obtain the invitations needed even to apply for emigration. Since authorities in a very few nations generally refuse to accept applications for exit permission without invitations, these few unfortunate persons are left with little or no legal channel through which to pursue efforts to exercise their rights as American citizens.

The intent of this proposal is not to force states to accept the concept of dual nationality formally. It is aimed only at stimulating them to accept the factual reality that some persons they consider to be their citizens are also accepted as citizens by another state and to allow those persons to choose for themselves which state they wish to reside in. The resolution of this handful of cases should not be difficult. To resolve these cases, the states involved are not being asked to alter any fundamental principle of their structure of rule, nor to open any flood-gate of claims. They are being asked only to deal in a humanitarian way with a handful of people who were actually born in another state or whose parents directly held citizenship of another state and transmitted it to their children. We appreciate the fact that over the past year one major participating state has favorably resolved several of these cases. In the same spirit, this proposal would help it to resolve expeditiously and favorably the handful of remaining cases.

Finally, I wish to speak in support of proposals BME 24 and 25, which are introduced by the delegation of France and which the United States is cosponsoring. The first of these proposals calls upon the participating states to recognize the right of their nationals to be issued a passport or any other document allowing travel abroad. The second obliges them to "abolish, for their nationals, the requirement to obtain an exit visa in order to leave their country."

Mr. Chairman, I will not repeat the lucid explanation offered by my distinguished French colleague in introducing these proposals. He spoke for my delegation as well. Instead, I would like to point to the fundamental principle underlying these proposals. It comes from the Universal Declaration of Human Rights, which affirms that "everyone has the right to leave any country, including his own, and to return." These two proposals recognize this solid and indisputable right. They help to define how this right may be exercised in fact, so that everyone actually can travel (except that small handful of cases, recognized by all countries, such as persons involved in criminal proceedings and minor children without the consent of their parents). These proposals reduce the barriers to such travel.

When a state makes the process of exit cumbersome and intimidating by requiring exit visas or by making passports difficult to obtain, it falls far short of international commitments. Specifically, it falls short of the letter and the spirit of the Final Act, in whose light proposals BME 24 and 25 have been advanced. According to these commitments, states must allow their people to choose for themselves whether to travel. All citizens should have in their hands the exit documents necessary to this right. The forward-looking steps being cautiously attempted as our dialogue in Bern has progressed offer us high hopes that these modest proposals will soon characterize not only most participating states but all participating states.

16
Extempore Reply: Administrative Labyrinths

MAY 6, 1986

MR. CHAIRMAN: My delegation is grateful for the list of questions posed by the distinguished delegate of the Soviet Union concerning BME 4, 5, and 6. This is the sort of mutual questioning and frank exchange that all of us wish to further. Nonetheless, the way in which the distinguished delegate of the Soviet Union phrased his question about BME 5 seemed quite disturbing. It brought to light a serious problem that is emerging in the CSCE process. This is the grievous problem of the difference that can open up between a commitment to principle and a commitment to the administrative execution of that principle. Usually we are able to take the connection between these two for granted, as simply a matter of good faith. Indeed, the distinguished delegate of Belgium just showed in his lucid way how the heads of state who signed the solemn commitments at the Helsinki Final Act and at Madrid intended to bind their countries both to the philosophical principles of the Final Act and to their administrative application in the real world.

As we saw again and again in our discussions in the plenary meetings, however, and as we are witnessing again and again in our discussions about proposals to advance the CSCE process, we have encountered a new and disturbing possibility. This is the possibility that a participating state might commit itself to the principles of the Helsinki Final Act and at the same time commit itself to frustrating their exercise. This frustration can be accomplished simply by changing the administrative regulations, so that what one offers with the one hand, one constantly takes away with the other. This leaves individuals vulnerable, baffled, and caught as in a nightmare. It has been a lesson of this terrible century that bureaucratic apparatus can put individuals in an impossible labyrinth, in a place of no exit, such as was described by the great existentialist "writers of the absurd," by Kafka, Sartre, Ionesco, and others, in metaphors so terrifyingly typical of our age. This was the horror pointed to just a moment ago by the distinguished delegate of Canada.

In short, Mr. Chairman, we are discovering the fertility of "the will to frustrate." It is quite possible that a state that does *not* wish to grant in fact what it has granted in principle will pursue endless bu-reaucratic evasions. Thus we encounter the possibility of a *will* on the part of a participating state *not* to become a more open society, a will to place a quarantine around human contacts, a will to frustrate—not to promote—human contacts.

Mr. Chairman, I hasten to add that openness is also a socialist ideal. There are in our midst a number of socialist states that are also open. We have heard a good many speeches around this table on the subject of socialist openness. Indeed, Secretary General Gorbachev has chosen those two words—"openness" and "transparency"—to de-scribe the administrative ideals of his regime, which is decidedly a socialist regime. Therefore, this question of openness does not point to a difference between socialist and nonsocialist systems. On the question of openness, both socialist and nonsocialist societies can be as one.

Mr. Chairman, I hope you will allow me to propose for my own further reflection, and for the attention of my colleagues, the dreadful possibility that all of us now face: the possibility of systematic *admin-istrative evasions* to frustrate the fundamental *principles* to which the heads of states of all our nations made a most solemn commitment. Here we face a real possibility, and we should understand its se-riousness. It *is* altogether possible for a participant state to eviscerate the philosophical principles of CSCE by frustrating them admin-istratively. If we allow this to happen, we are all engaged in a great illusion, a systematic evasion, a dance of pure fakery.

In order to block this new danger, many delegations in this room have now been forced to take the step, which should not be necessary, of translating the *philosophical principles of the Final Act into admin-istrative principles*, to prevent such evasion.

Thus, in BME 5, for example, care has been taken to specify the length of time applications for exit visas would remain valid, and in other proposals we have also specified the time during which certain things must be done, and so forth. This translation of philosophical principles into administrative principles ought not to be necessary, if all were proceeding in good faith.

Therefore, Mr. Chairman, I would like to call the attention of my colleagues to the seriousness of what we are now doing. Virtually all our proposals merely translate philosophical principles into admin-istrative principles. This does not really advance the argument very much, but it is necessary. If we fail in this task, if we fail in this translation from philosophical principles into administrative princi-ples, we will fail to meet the challenge that Sir Alex Douglas-Home set before us eleven years ago, which I mentioned in my opening address. We will fail to translate the beautiful philosophical principles of the Final Act, which inspired so much hope around the world, into the administrative realities that make life better for ordinary people everywhere.

17
Removing Legal Obstacles
Restricting Contacts

MAY 7, 1986

MR. CHAIRMAN: I would like to introduce proposal BME 13, cosponsored by the delegations of Canada, the Federal Republic of Germany, and the Netherlands. The operative section of this proposal calls upon the participating states to "remove legal and other obstacles restricting or inhibiting contacts on their own territory between their citizens and resident or visiting citizens of other states."

Mr. Chairman, in view of the conviction expressed by the participating states in the Final Act that "the development of contacts [is] . . . an important element in the strengthening of friendly relations and trust among peoples," this modest proposal may at first seem unnecessary. States that so solemnly affirmed the importance of human contacts, it was expected, would promptly remove those legal and administrative measures that had inhibited their citizens from freely meeting with foreign visitors. It is, indeed, a rude surprise to find that in the years since the Final Act—in one or two participating states—*new* and harsher restrictions have been imposed. Sadly, several participating states have not, in fact, gone forward to encourage a greater degree of human interaction. They have stepped backward. Proposal BME 13 is therefore necessary to recover lost ground. It merely spells out what the Final Act took for granted.

One of the most blatant of the new laws restricting human contacts was introduced by a participating state on May 25, 1984. This law has been questioned several times already in this conference. It makes citizens liable to fines of a considerable sum (given that nation's median income) simply for violating so-called "rules of stay . . . by foreign citizens or stateless persons." The decree specifies other fines for citizens who provide foreigners with "housing or means of transportation or . . . other services in violation of the established regulations."

Alas, only the authorities of that state know precisely what "the established regulations" really are. The effect of this decree is to discourage contacts between citizens and foreign visitors. It quaran-

---

Delivered extempore from notes and reconstructed from notes.

tines visitors, separating them from ordinary citizens. These citizens are prevented from inviting foreign visitors to stay overnight in their homes without the required preliminary registration with authorities. Citizens are prevented from providing foreigners with other services such as the use of a car or assistance in purchasing train or airline tickets. Their natural feelings of hospitality are stifled. Their natural urge for open human contacts is repressed. Their natural curiosity and openness are blocked.

The broad wording of the regulation of May 25, 1984, makes it applicable in any situation in which the authorities wish to prevent "unauthorized" contact either with foreign tourists or with officially sanctioned professional visitors. The reference to "stateless persons" seems to be intended to include a category of persons who have renounced their citizenship, a necessary condition in applying for emigration, and who have not yet been allowed to leave. In order to emigrate, the law obliges them to become stateless, and by refusing them permission to leave, authorities keep them so.

Another new law that aims at limiting contacts between foreigners and citizens is the law of the same participating state, on the legal status of foreign visitors, passed in June 1981. This law consolidated and codified a number of existing practices. Its effect was to subject foreigners to the same legal and extralegal constraints that apply to that state's citizens. It gives the authorities broad discretionary power to prevent contact between foreigners and citizen activists, both civil and religious.

Under this law those found guilty of transgressing "rules of the socialist community [or] the traditions and customs of the . . . people" may be detained to face criminal charges or be expelled. Given the explicit commitments made by heads of state at Helsinki and foreign ministers at Madrid, these "rules" and "traditions and customs" *should* by now have been examined in the light of international commitments. But, alas, they are not even clearly spelled out.

Not all restrictions on contacts between foreigners and citizens of that state are established in law or regulation. Some are enforced by other mechanisms. For example, foreign journalists, commercial representatives, students, and other resident foreigners must provide advance notification to the government of all planned travel beyond the immediate area where they reside. In practice, they must also book transportation and lodging through government agencies. Both of these mechanisms are regularly used by those agencies to control travel.

In few countries are human contacts so deliberately obstructed. For example, the authorities of that state officially announce that 80 percent of their nation is open to foreigners. Most foreigners visiting or traveling there, however, must make travel arrangements, including accommodations, through the state travel agency. They may use only government-approved facilities. And these government-approved facilities provide access to only approximately 5 percent of the territory of that state. Thus vast stretches of that country are off-limits to foreigners. No other participating state is so restrictive. The vast majority of participating states permit far more open travel without official permission, allowing nonofficial visitors to make their own arrangements freely.

Contacts between foreigners and citizens in that state are further limited since foreigners are usually required to stay in officially sanctioned hotels and citizens of that country who do not have official permission find it difficult to enter such hotels. Guards are stationed outside to keep ordinary citizens away, lest one of them seek "unauthorized" contact with a foreigner. Tragically, these restrictions at times prevent meetings between foreign visitors and their own relatives. These restrictions make visitors feel quite odd, like carriers of a virus. They are human beings not allowed to come in genuine person-to-person contact with other human beings.

Mr. Chairman, the need for this proposal is not limited to one nation. Allow me to describe the situation in two other Eastern European states. In one of these states several decrees affecting contact with foreigners are not published but do have the full force of law. It is in fact against the law to mention these decrees to foreigners. Of course, some citizens speak out anyway. Thus most of the countries here with diplomatic missions in that country know about these decrees. One such law requires that every contact with a foreigner, whether official or private, whether planned or coincidental, must be reported to the police within twenty-four hours. Recently this decree has been extended to require *prior* approval, in certain cases, from the police or other authority.

Other laws in this same country, some published, some not, forbid an individual to offer his home as lodging to a foreigner, even for a friendly overnight visit, unless there is a close family relationship. "Close relationship" is even defined in the law to mean only parent, child, or sibling.

Finally, this same country has a vibrant religious life and in the past used to allow open contacts between its people and their co-religionists from other countries. Now there come shocking reports of a new decree forbidding religious ministers from foreign countries from preaching in this country's churches. We will return to this topic at a later point.

Let me also describe how the second Eastern European state has discouraged human contacts even further. In that country the so-called contacts prohibition applies to millions of people, or more than 10 percent of its population, on the basis of their employment. To those in this category, all contact with foreign citizens from the West is simply forbidden. They are not allowed to make or receive international phone calls, to send or receive international post, to engage in casual conversation with visitors to their country, or even to retain their seat in a restaurant if a westerner happens to sit at that table. These rules apply not only to that state's extensive security service but to ordinary people, including firemen, some teachers, the custodial staff of military or security establishments, and near and distant relatives of people who might have some casual contact with the broad range of items defined by that state as "state secrets." To give just one example, an elderly man was forbidden to visit his relatives in the Federal Republic of Germany because his *children* were employed by a shipyard. Ten percent—or more—of the population; no other country so completely cuts off foreign contact for such a large proportion of its own citizens.

On the other hand, my delegation takes pleasure in acknowledging that several states that used to be significantly closed have, under the stimulus of the Final Act, returned to the normal human openness dictated by common sense. Socialism, they find, is quite compatible with openness. They now permit considerably greater interaction between their citizens and visiting foreigners than they did a decade or so ago. From their commitment to common sense they have reaped significant rewards, not so much in the esteem in which sister states hold them—although that, too, is a precious good—as in the improved morale and energy of their own people. For their greater degree of openness, they have not been penalized; on the contrary, they have gained a great deal, internally and externally.

Thus there are powerful reasons to hope that the *very* few nations still fearful of open human contacts, perhaps because of sad experiences, will now also experiment in the ways of openness and transparency and thus fulfill their obligations under the Final Act and the Madrid Concluding Document. Our own delegation hopes that the adoption of this small and obvious proposal will help break down some of those barriers, old and new, that have been erected to limit human contacts. Its adoption would do much to restore the credibility of CSCE commitments and to build genuine confidence among peoples and between states. All Europe would be a happier place.

18
Religious and Human Contacts
MAY 7, 1986

MR. CHAIRMAN: I would like to speak today on a proposal that has not yet been officially introduced, BME 26. More exactly, I would like to speak about some of the important concepts that lie behind it. Much has changed in the field of religion since the Second World War, especially because international contacts have grown much closer. In universities throughout the world today, anybody who would teach courses about religion faces questions seldom faced before. In a contemporary university the meaning of "religion" is necessarily different from what it was in the nineteenth century or at any earlier time. It must be supposed that the authors of the Helsinki document intended their words to have contemporary relevance. They must have known that, today, when scholars use the word "religion," they must take into account all the various phenomena from around the world that are sometimes described under that title. Consider the following examples:

• When one uses the word "religion," is one speaking about a church? But some religions in the world are quite antichurch and anti-institutional.

• When one uses the word "religion," is one speaking about theology? But some religions of the world are quite antitheological, anticonceptual, antipropositional.

• When one uses the word "religion," is one speaking about inwardness? But some religions in the world have a powerful social doctrine and speak directly to the questions of politics, economics, peace, and other social issues.

• When one uses the word "religion," is one speaking of theism? But some religions in the world do not use the name of God, and some even claim to be nondeist, preferring to speak of nothingness, or emptiness, abnegation, and the like.

Thus in speaking of religion within a contemporary world view, one must keep in mind not only Hinduism, Islam, Buddhism, Judaism, Christianity, Shinto, and Confucianism but even all those totally secular ideologies that place each person within a social story, giving meaning to history and to individual life—including such secular ideologies as Marxism. Many scholars point out that Karl Marx deliberately designed several basic principles of Marxist philosophy around key conceptions of apocalyptic Christianity. Like other ideologies, Marxism attempts to give meaning to history, has its own ethic, and claims a universal scope. All such systems, these days, must also be treated in universities as forms of secular religion.

Second, Mr. Chairman, there is another dimension of change characteristic of our time: In our day human contacts occur on a planetary scale. They involve the meeting of stranger with stranger, the meeting of culture with culture. Hardly anyone these days is unaware that others in the world are different. Almost everywhere we see the interpenetration of ways of looking at the world, of stories and images concerning the meaning of history. Peoples, whatever their own faith, today know and meet others who are of different faiths. In our time human contacts are international in scope and bring about the clash of many differences in how individuals see the world, understand themselves, and understand their own relationship to one another and to history.

This in fact is what is most human about us—our capacity for self-reflection. In contact with alternatives, we are capable of *self-discovery*, in whose light we see ourselves differently from the way we ever did before. We are capable of *self-invention*, once we see from others that we do not have to live as we are now living but could choose to live rather differently.

Mr. Chairman, this is where the two concepts of religion and human contacts come together. Human contacts on a planetary scale force each human being to raise questions about the way in which he or she is now living, now imagines himself or herself, and now comes to some understanding of what it means to live as a human being. Such questions are universal. In a universal sense they are today what is meant by religion. These questions come more rapidly and with greater power precisely because of the *international* scope of human contacts in our time.

For this reason, Mr. Chairman, persons concerned about such questions, religious persons in a universal sense, have a profound need of contacts with others. They need contacts with books, narratives, autobiographies, confessions, the records of the voyages taken by other human beings. To be a human being today is to share in the questions faced by others and to see how and why one is different from others. One needs contact with others, in order to question one's own consciousness. Thus in our time religion is best characterized as a voyage—exploratory, never ending. This voyage is at once *personal*, in the depths of consciousness, and *social*, in contact with all other human beings. This voyage is what distinguishes human beings from all the other animals and from every other known phenomenon. It is what makes us *human*. This voyage today can be as well informed as it has the possibility of becoming only by contact with all others.

Therefore, Mr. Chairman, when the Final Act speaks of religion and of human contacts, it is speaking of two things each of which is essential to the other. What make contacts truly *human* are the questions they raise for each person about his or her voyage through life, as it is affected by others. In this way religion, in the broad sense in which I have been using the term, concerns a personal and social *voyage* of great importance to being human—and, simultaneously, very much in need of human *contacts* from person to person, society to society. To strangle religion, to deprive it of books, to deprive its participants of rights to travel and to receive mail and to acquire materials, is to strangle both what is human and the importance of contacts among humans, in helping each person to grow into his or her full possibilities in such an international world as ours.

Mr. Chairman, I would like to introduce one other concept. That is the question of national minorities. Our world today is a world of minorities. Each person is born from the belly of a single woman, into a single language, into a single culture. Each of us belongs to a single minority on this planet. Yet we have heard much in our meetings already about the sufferings of a variety of minorities upon this planet. At this point, then, I would like to recall the ideals behind the Final Act. I would like to read a wise text of a patriot of his own minority and a protector of other minorities. This text was delivered as a speech to a national assembly forty-six years ago, but it reminds us of the principles on which the Final Act is built.

In 1940 Bulgaria was under grievous pressure from National Socialists under Hitler. Some fanatics tried to rush through a "law for the protection of the nation." This was a law meant to define Jews as threats to the nation and to make them vulnerable—to what? to destruction. Such was the ferocity against minorities, when a former leader of that country and a member of Parliament rose to speak. Permit me to read the words that he delivered on November 19, 1940:

> As a matter of fact, life in our country confirms that our state is a national state, in spite of the fact that on Bulgarian territory there exist also other nationalities and other religions. Jews, Turks, Romanians, Greeks, A.O. [and others]. Never, however, have these alien elements given us reason to question the national character of our state. On the con-

trary. All these groups with different religion and of different nationality taken together have never, in any way, challenged the national character of the Bulgarian State. This is something which we have to acknowledge before we start to look for the reasons which have prompted the government to track down the enemies of the nation and to suggest measures for the protection against these enemies.

The creators of our law of the laws, the Tirnovo Constitution, never considered the people professing other religions or of other nationality as elements, which are anti-national in relation to the state in which they live. Therefore, nowhere in the Constitution, whenever human rights and general rights are mentioned, is any kind of distinction made among the different nationalities living in our country. Every citizen of Bulgaria enjoys the same rights. And on this fact rests our strength.

Let me remind you that during the era of Karavelov the gypsies were deprived of their rights. This provoked a public uproar and the National Assembly, under the pressure of public opinion, had to restore to the gypsies their constitutional rights. The vigilant national feeling did not admit any discrimination.

I have governed this country. I have always been a proud Bulgarian, proud to belong to a people which always has respected principle, respected the human being and guaranteed it every possibility for free development. I have always been able to confront foreigners with pride when I defended the cause of the Bulgarians living beyond the borders of our state, and when I could tell them that I live in a country, that I am the son of a people which tolerates on its soil the existence of other religions, of other nationalities, which respects the human being also in its adversary.

The "law for the protection of the nation" never came into effect. Under pressure of public opinion and after the intervention of the National Assembly and the king, the Bulgarian Jews were saved from deportation.

Mr. Chairman, it is obvious that this text has relevance to discussions we have heard in our meetings. It is sometimes important to remember that the words of one eloquent and brave man can have a powerful effect upon history. Because of this speech and because of the intervention of the Bulgarian king, the "law for the protection of the nation" was not passed. And the Jews of Bulgaria were not destroyed, as earlier before them the gypsies had begun to be destroyed.

Mr. Chairman, we are all minorities. It is well to recall from time to time that the suffering that befalls one minority soon befalls another and then another. Therefore, each of us has an interest in protecting every minority.

It is well for each of us to remember that a brave man, a patriot, once spoke up to defend a minority endangered in his own country, thus to defend the honor of the minority in this world to which he himself belonged.

Thank you, Mr. Chairman.

19
Extempore Right of Reply on Labor Unions

[After an emotional attack by Victor Shikalov of the Soviet delegation upon the history of labor in the United States.]

MR. CHAIRMAN: I would like, through you, to thank the distinguished delegate of the USSR for his emotional remarks. Heated debate, too, is a form of human contact.

I would like to thank him, as well, for setting an admirable example: he has been able not only to offer his own proposals but also to attack those made by others. Some of the rest of us have been working so hard simply to present our own proposals that we are not quite ready to discuss all the proposals (more than forty now) that have been falling like the snowflakes of two or three weeks ago. I would like to assure the distinguished delegate of the USSR that my delegation will soon have many questions about the Soviet proposals.

Third, I would like to thank the distinguished delegate of the USSR for mentioning at one point "the wonderful USA." [Laughter] Amid his biting remarks, that phrase touched a warm spot. [Laughter] As for myself, I would not have been bold enough to say it. Ours is a country like any other. A big country, it has perhaps big faults. But one thing I like about our country, for which I am grateful that my grandparents long ago moved to it and made me its citizen, is that we keep plugging away at our faults, trying as best we can to correct them.

I would like to thank the distinguished delegate of the USSR, further, for strengthening my case. In stressing the air traffic controllers and other state employees, both of whom have the state as their employer, he helped to show why we in the United States do somewhat distrust the state. He perhaps sees now why we make a rather sharp distinction between labor unions that have the state as an employer and free trade unions in the normal sense of the term. In our country those who work for the state have a no-strike clause in their contracts, which they sign upon employment. This clause binds them both in law and in conscience.

And for good reason. Consider the air traffic controllers. Each of them had signed a no-strike clause. Suppose they had gone on strike. Imagine, then, the air space over LaGuardia Airport, over Kennedy Airport, over O'Hare Airport, and over Atlanta Airport—all among the busiest in the world. With no air traffic controllers on the job, these would have been lively places [laughter]—both on the ground and in the air. In that case there were reasons for prohibiting a strike, reasons both of public safety and of contracts binding both in law and in conscience.

I would like to thank the distinguished delegate of the USSR, as well, for bringing up the Taft-Hartley Act. As he mentioned, that complex law is now more than thirty years old. I am not a lawyer, and it would certainly take a lawyer to explain all its provisions, since it has been amended so many times. I am sorry that you have to rely on me, since we have so many lawyers in the United States that we have a saying: if you took all the lawyers and laid them end to end, on the whole it would probably be a good thing. [Much laughter] Today, alas, we will have to proceed without a lawyer. Still, there are two points about Taft-Hartley I can make.

First, freedom does not mean lawlessness. Like other free citizens, so also trade unions live under the law. Why? Because it is also the law that *protects* them. Law and liberty go together. We believe, in our phrase, in "liberty under law."

Second, one feature of the Taft-Hartley Act, sometimes helpful, sometimes painful, is that under certain conditions it permits the declaration of a ninety-day cooling-off period, during which collective bargaining may continue. If that is not successful, then the right to strike again comes into force. These conditions include public safety and a good that is national in scope, such as transportation.

The distinguished delegate of the USSR mentioned transportation workers, medical workers, teachers in the public schools, and some others as not being able to strike. He is wrong in detail, but note that these are professions that may affect the public safety or the public good. Thus, implicitly, he makes the point that the right to strike must be made consistent with other rights and that these various rights sometimes come into conflict. For this reason, as he noted in a derogatory way in several remarks, recourse is often had to the courts. In our country courts are independent and highly prized. Sometimes labor unions, sometimes their individual members, and sometimes other members of the public appeal to them to protect their own rights in competition with the rights of others. The courts must then adjudicate among rights.

Next, I must note that in listening to the picture of U.S. labor history given by the distinguished delegate of the Soviet Union, one would never know that there have been successful strikes, one would never learn of the immense strides forward in living standards made possible by the activities of our labor unions, and one would never know of the high pay scales achieved by our labor unions in certain industries, such that, counting benefits, some individual workers may be being paid as much as $30 an hour.

Indeed, one of the loveliest bits of U.S. history, too often neglected, is the history of labor. Since my own field is philosophy and theology, the distinguished delegate of the Soviet Union could have had no way of knowing that at one point in my life I wrote a book on the history of the United Mine Workers, concerning the great strike of 1897, a strike conducted mostly by Slavic workers, speaking Slavic languages, and for that reason long neglected by historians—a strike that failed in its immediate context but that led within seven years to the intervention of the president of the United States, Theodore Roosevelt, not on the side of the mine owners but on the side of the miners. The history of American labor unions is a lively history. In our country, Mr. Chairman, freedom means conflict. We think of this as "creative conflict." This is why our labor unionists so greatly love liberty.

Finally, Mr. Chairman, although, regretfully, I *was* away on April 27 and 28, when the distinguished delegate of the Soviet Union last spoke on labor unions, I must note that in our time human contacts do not always require one's physical presence. On each day of my absence (during which I missed all of you), I received copies of the speeches given here, and in particular the speeches of the distinguished delegate of the USSR, on the very day they were given. I read them intently.

I recall reading in one of them, or perhaps in a speech given by his colleague a little after, the allegation that an American trade unionist named (as I believe I heard) Jim Perry, from the firefighters' union in Los Angeles, made derogatory comments about the United States on a visit to Moscow on May Day. The impression was given here that this was May Day 1986, unless I misunderstood the text, but in truth Mr. Perry went to Moscow in 1985. His group was not allowed to deviate from the official schedule, not even to visit a firehouse they were passing, which Mr. Perry would have liked to visit to see his fellow firefighters at work. When he returned to the United States, Mr. Perry was sent a copy of a Novosti press release containing the derogatory comments allegedly made by him. No such interview took place. Mr. Perry denied ever making such statements. He wrote a

103

letter to the Soviet embassy in Washington, protesting these statements falsely attributed to him. He still has not received a reply from the Soviet embassy, now a little more than a year later.

I apologize for speaking on these matters, beyond our mandate, Mr. Chairman. But in such circumstances each delegation has the right to reply, and it seemed to me to be my obligation to set the record straight. Now, if you will permit me, I will return to my prepared remarks, in support of the proposal on nongovernmental organizations.

[Ambassador Novak here turned to his prepared text, as follows.]

20
In Support of Free Labor Unions
MAY 8, 1986

MR. CHAIRMAN: It has sometimes been argued during our frank dialogue that there is an unbridgeable chasm between the individual and the organized mass, between individualism and collectivism. My delegation flatly rejects that view. For example, today we introduce BME 15 (On Contacts between Free Labor Unions) and speak in cosponsorship of BME 7 (On Contacts between Non-Governmental Organizations). Both free labor unions and nongovernmental organizations are mediating institutions. They stand *between* the individual and the state. They are *social* in nature, not individualist. They are *associational*, not collectivist.

These mediating institutions are crucial to a fully human life. The individual cannot long live in isolation, apart from human community. Genuine human community depends upon the choice of free individual persons, persons of conscience and concern for others, who have learned the spirit of cooperation and teamwork.

It is not true, Mr. Chairman, that in order to work as one, human beings need to be organized from the top down, through the state. Human beings are cooperative animals. They are free animals who rejoice in voluntarily joining together in smoothly operating teams. We see metaphors for this simultaneous reliance in great public sports events. Millions admire the unique talents and free spontaneous choices of each individual player; they know the names of each, but the millions also admire smooth cooperation in team play—in European football and North American baseball, in hockey and in basketball, and in other sports. These public liturgies of sport touch some of the most profound human instincts of ordinary people everywhere. Human beings spontaneously admire both extraordinary individuals and teamwork.

On the one side, every individual is extraordinary, unique, irrepeatable. No two persons are alike. On the other side, every individual is also social, enjoys the company of others, and delights in conquering difficult tasks in unity with a willing band of others. Of these, Shakespeare wrote four centuries ago: "We few, we happy few, we band of brothers."

So it is, Mr. Chairman, with labor unions. Free labor unions are

105

voluntary associations, formed from the bottom up, not the top down. They arise from a multitude of individual choices, through which hundreds or thousands or even millions of individuals through their own separate free choices band themselves together.

Mr. Chairman, our delegation favors human systems, whether of socialist or "mixed" economies, that promote a broad, deep social life, rooted in human liberty, rich in the practice of free association. That is why we take pleasure in cosponsoring, with the distinguished delegations of Belgium and Canada, BME 15. This small proposal, already observed by a vast majority of participating states but always in need of nourishment and increased support everywhere, calls upon the participating states to "remove existing impediments which prevent freely established trade unions, their members and their representatives from maintaining contact, communications and organizational ties with similar organizations in other participating states without need of official sponsorship or approval."

Mr. Chairman, the goal of this proposal is to improve the prospect for contacts between free trade unions, their representatives, and members as called for in the Madrid Concluding Document. In determining whether a trade union is freely established, definitions under appropriate International Labor Organization (ILO) conventions and recommendations are instructive. Critical criteria are the right of association and the rights to organize and bargain collectively. The right of association has been defined by the ILO in four steps, which include the rights of workers and employers (1) to establish and join organizations of their own choosing, without previous authorization; (2) to draft their own constitutions and rules; (3) freely to elect their own representatives and formulate their own programs; and (4) to join confederations and to affiliate or to refrain from affiliating with international organizations of their own choosing.

Thus free trade unions are crucial mediating structures. They are not state controlled; their origin lies in the free choice of individuals. They are not collectivist, like bees in a hive or cattle in a herd; they are associational, the natural expression of the human being's free preference for joining together freely to accomplish tasks too large to be accomplished by any one individual alone.

Some will ask, How can there be rational order, unless there are a few to give orders from above? How can there be unity if millions of individuals have free choice? How can a society escape anarchy without coercion? Long ago Shakespeare showed how things disparate and individual, things that seem to work contrariously, may freely end in blessed unity. He wrote (in *King Henry V*, Act I, sc. 2):

Many things, having full reference
To one consent, may work contrariously;
As many arrows, loosed several ways,
Fly to one mark; as many ways meet in one town;
As many fresh streams meet in one salt sea;
As many lines close in the dial's center;
So may a thousand actions, once afoot,
End in one purpose, and be all well borne
Without defeat.

Alas, in a very few participating states, the criteria for free labor unions set forth by the ILO have not yet been met in practice. Laws and practices in such states simply do not allow for the creation and functioning of freely established trade unions. The formation of unions through voluntary human contacts, in accord with the universal human right to free association, is not allowed to be exercised in practice. In those few states, not only is the state the only or the principal employer; it is also the only collective representative of the employees. Between employer and employees there is no mediating institution—no check upon absolute power, no counterbalance.

In such participating states, the primary responsibility of trade union officials is to government (and party) rather than to the workers. A Czechoslovak newspaper stated this point clearly when it wrote:

The relationship between trade unions and the state is always determined by who owns the means of production and whose instrument is the state which protects that ownership. In the conditions of real socialism the slogan of the so-called independent trade union is nothing but a deception. It is always reactionary. It is, in fact, aimed at weakening the main instrument for building an advanced socialist society, the socialist state.

According to this doctrine, unions independent of state control and state interests have no right to exist.

Harsh experience in the past decade has shown that the governments of some participating states do ruthlessly suppress any attempt to form independent unions, abolish them, often imprison their leaders and members, and try by all means to prevent them from organizing in the first place. One of the measures used against such organizations and persons is to cut them off from contact with persons and organizations abroad, especially free trade unions elsewhere. There are, unfortunately, many concrete examples that must be cited:

- In 1984 United Auto Workers International representative John Christenson was told by the Polish embassy in Washington that he would not be granted a visa to visit Poland if his visit would include any meetings with Solidarity members. A further condition, he was told, would be that upon arrival he must publicly acknowledge the official trade union (OPZZ) as the sole legitimate workers' organization. In view of these conditions, he did not proceed with a formal application for a visa.

- In 1985 Christenson was invited to visit the Soviet Union. Upon indicating he would seek out representatives of SMOT, the suppressed independent Soviet trade union, he was orally informed by the Soviet authorities that a visa would not be issued. Again, no formal application or denial occurred.

- In 1977 the AFL-CIO, the largest association of free trade unionists in the world, invited six Soviet citizens (including four dissident free trade unionists and the widow of another) to attend the 1977 AFL-CIO biannual convention. The invitations were tampered with en route, and exit visas were denied.

- In 1981 and again in 1983 Lech Walesa was invited to the AFL-CIO conventions. He withdrew his applications for exit visas when the Polish government refused to assure him that he would be allowed to return to Poland.

- At the time Solidarity was still legal in Poland, it invited AFL-CIO president Lane Kirkland to attend its founding Congress. The Polish government refused him a visa.

Mr. Chairman, adoption and implementation of this proposal would mean that free trade unionists around the world would be able to receive visas from Eastern countries to visit, as they choose, free trade unionists in those countries. It would also mean that when they invite such free trade unionists to visit them, the latter would be permitted by right and by normal practice to accept the invitations. This is only common sense and common practice, no more than that.

As things now stand, the only trade unionists permitted by many East European regimes to travel or to receive visits are those "official" unionists who are, in the eyes of free U.S. trade unionists, merely government representatives. Were those East European regimes to permit freedom of contacts and travel for *all* trade unionists, including those associated with unions or workers' groups unconnected to official unions, our free trade unionists have said that they would certainly reconsider their current insistence that U.S. law remain as it is regarding the representatives of official trade unions in certain Communist states.

American free trade unionists regard official unions in Communist states as instruments of the state, the sole or principal employer, not as true expressions of the free choice of individual members. They would, however, delightedly welcome genuinely free associations of trade unionists of any ideology or country. The tests our free trade unionists apply are two: genuine liberty of association, including the right to strike and to achieve collective bargaining; and reciprocity. This last point, reciprocity, is covered in the words of BME 15 in this way: "The right to maintain contact, communication and organizational ties with similar organizations in other participating states without need of official sponsorship or approval."

Mr. Chairman, the support by consensus of the small step forward recommended in BME 15 would do wonders to generate abundant human contacts between free trade unionists in our country and those in every other participating state. The American people and American free trade unionists would deeply welcome that.

[Next part delivered later in same meeting]

21
In Support of Nongovernmental Organizations

MAY 8, 1986

MR. CHAIRMAN: My delegation is also a cosponsor of proposal BME 7, which was introduced earlier by my distinguished Danish colleague. This proposal deals with contacts between nongovernmental organizations and institutions in the various participating states.

Mr. Chairman, my delegation's earlier comments, quite rightly, focused on contacts between individuals and especially between members of the most basic social unit, the family. Human beings are social animals—but social animals each of whom is free and responsible. All contacts between human beings that are fully human respect both sides of human nature: the social side and free individual choice. Thus many delegations here in Bern have rightly emphasized that human contacts must, to the maximum extent possible, originate in the choices of the individuals involved, not in the state or any other collective unit. On the other side, individuals often and normally act together, in social institutions, not as Robinson Crusoes. (That, in fact, is how all of us here in Bern are proceeding: although each individual among us is unique, we cooperate together as a common body.) Recognizing the natural human instinct for association, for cooperation, for teamwork, my delegation is happy to cosponsor proposal BME 7, to expand the scope for free associations arising from individual choice and independent of government.

Mr. Chairman, mediating institutions of this sort are crucial to the enhancement of human energy. Alone, individuals can do comparatively little; together they can do great things. But human beings are naturally far more energetic when they are cooperating freely, of their own choice, doing what they *want* to do. When they work freely, as a team, individuals have strength far beyond their individual strength alone. Free association is the first law of the new science of politics, Alexis de Tocqueville brilliantly argued 150 years ago. History has proved him right. Individuals operating only in collectives need constant exhortation from above. Individuals acting in teams that they have freely chosen display remarkable energy, exceeding by far such energy as they might summon up alone.

Nonetheless, with this proposal, BME 7, our delegation is not seeking complete substitution of contacts between nongovernmental or unofficial groups for those between officially sponsored or approved organizations. While we strongly believe that contacts between private individuals and mediating institutions best promote human contact and mutual understanding, we recognize that other, less personal contacts between organizations of all types also have some place. We regret that some participating states permit *only* officially approved organizations to exist. Contacts between those groups and foreign organizations are tightly controlled. Attempts at contacts on the part of "unapproved" organizations take place only at great hazard to the persons involved, if at all.

The fostering of mutual understanding among peoples requires that all shades of opinion be encountered. It is good, even necessary, for our peoples to be exposed to the widest possible variety of human expression. An officially sponsored or approved organization generally expresses official views. It is desirable that the peoples of our countries have the opportunity to hear such views. It is also essential that our peoples, on all levels, be able to deal directly with persons and organizations that offer different, nonofficial, eyes-open, and critical perspectives.

Governments of all kinds like to project a favorable image of themselves. Some of the distinguished delegations among our cherished colleagues here who are most critical of my own country would no doubt agree with me on one point. Their own files on the failures and shortcomings of the United States would be far thinner if they had to rely solely on what the U.S. government says about itself and about American society. Indeed, a high proportion of what those states permit their peoples to know about the United States originates in the free press and among nongovernmental organizations in the United States that are critical of various aspects of American society. Thank God, these nongovernmental organizations express this criticism freely and communicate with persons and organizations in other states at will.

Nongovernmental organizations keep governments honest. Governments generally need that. Nongovernmental organizations often generate new ideas, imagine new horizons, and help to shape the agenda of the future. If you will allow me to speak as a theologian, I would say that humans working freely together as a team are images of God—and for this reason alone it is no surprise that they are often so creative. States without such organizations are punished, comparatively, by lethargy.

Mr. Chairman, the second part of proposal BME 7 deals with a more specific problem. Sometimes a person from one country invited by an organization of another country to come to an event in the latter is suddenly replaced by a person not invited at all. Rather frequently an organization has invited a person from one or another Eastern European country to attend an event. The person accepts the invitation. At the last minute, the person originally invited is told by his government that he or she cannot go. Without the consent of the inviting organization, another person is sent in the invitee's place. It has happened on occasion that the substitute is by no means desired by the inviting organization. This part of BME 7 is aimed at restoring common courtesy, common liberty, and common respect for one another's wishes.

We think BME 7 is a sensible proposal that will profoundly and deeply enhance genuine human contacts.

22
Religious Contacts

by Ambassador Sol Polansky

MAY 9, 1986

MR. CHAIRMAN: Much of what we have discussed during the implementation review phase is what has been called by some "individual contacts," as opposed to mass contacts. Today I would like to discuss a kind of contact that may be considered as falling in the category of mass contacts but is in fact of the most personal and intimate importance to the individual: religious contacts.

The United States is a country that strictly separates the state from the church and zealously guards the rights of nonbelievers as well as believers. Still, organized religion and personal belief flourish in my country. Name any religion that exists in the world, and I can almost guarantee that you will find that faith's adherents active in the United States. So religious contacts cannot be a matter of indifference to us. A broad range of contacts across borders brings challenge, inspiration, and cooperation to religious individuals and organizations. For the individual it is often a key ingredient of his devotion to God, his service to man, his perception of a higher truth or reality.

The importance that people of all cultures attach to their individual beliefs is seen in the vigorous demonstrations of religious observance in countries where the right to such observance cannot be taken for granted. It is in order to connect these people of disparate cultures, including religiously rooted cultures, to show the unity of man despite the diversity of systems, that the participating states in the CSCE process accepted the commitment to foster such contacts among religious organizations and faiths across borders.

Together with other delegations represented here, the U.S. delegation seeks improved compliance with the letter and intent of this commitment. To understand the pertinency and even urgency of the issue, consider the actual situation regarding religious contacts in a number of CSCE signatory countries.

Please note in this connection that the Madrid Concluding Document states that the signatories "will further implement" the relevant provisions of the Final Act. Unfortunately, this obligation has not been taken to heart in certain countries. In six of the participating states religious believers are today in jail for the mere transporting of reli-

113

gious materials. Strict border controls on the transport of Bibles and other religious material have frustrated the Concluding Document's provision that religious organizations be allowed to exchange information. Possessing imported Bibles is defined in one participating state as "illegal distribution of literature" and deemed a criminal offense. This same government refuses to allow any legal import of Bibles, although religious communities in that country have confirmed the need for hundreds of thousands of Bibles for their members. Aware of this desire, their coreligionists in the West arranged to donate Bibles. Another specific example that merits attention is the following: in Czechoslovakia in 1985, I regret to say, three Catholic Slovaks were sentenced to terms ranging from thirty-two to sixty-six months for attempting to import religious materials from another Eastern European country. Some may say that those individuals technically violated laws on smuggling, but in their own minds they were clearly exercising the right they thought was guaranteed them by the Madrid Concluding Document, the right to exchange religious materials with other communities of believers.

Mr. Chairman, the Bible was perhaps the first great manifesto for personal liberation. It is dismaying that some governments treat the most widely published book in the world as a subversive tract, threatening to national security or the social structure of the state. The Bible is merely an indispensable element of the right of belief nominally guaranteed by the constitutions of these same states. Guaranteeing someone religious freedom without allowing him to read a Bible or any other religious work important to his conscience is a meaningless freedom. To prevent the importation of the Bible is, as Ambassador Novak stressed on May 6, a clear example of the use of administrative measures to frustrate the philosophical principles at the heart of the Final Act, solemnly signed by the heads of state of the CSCE participating states.

Nor can hard currency shortages be invoked in this context as an excuse for preventing such imports. There are numerous private organizations in the West prepared to meet the palpable demand for Bibles in some countries of Eastern Europe. The authorities in these countries claim there is no "demand" for Bibles in their countries. If that is indeed the case, those authorities should certainly have no difficulty in allowing their citizens to make that choice themselves.

I do not mean to imply that Bibles are the only important items of religious literature exchanged by religious organizations. A multitude of creative works from all faiths is an essential part of this process. In a kind of cross-fertilization, the different faiths of the world can contribute to the broad consciousness of man and to his longing for personal fulfillment. A government that shows itself afraid of having its citizens share in religious philosophy or activity is a government that deprives its people of a potential source of inspiration, feeling, perception, and commitment.

The exchange of information is, of course, just one example of religious human contacts. Another example is direct contact between religious believers, and that should also be our focus today. Most of the governments represented here, including some in Eastern Europe, permit free and unhindered travel for believers, whether they are traveling in groups or singly, as part of a private or communal mission. But others are not so generous in spirit. One government, with an Islamic population constituting 10 percent of its citizens, is currently in the process of changing the names of those citizens and restricting traditional religious practices, such as certain burial rites. What could be more mean-spirited, since these rites have as their purpose the comforting of grieving family members and loved ones. Since 1944 that government has permitted only a handful of its citizens to undertake the most holy duty of a devout Muslim, a pilgrimage to Mecca.

Several Slavic countries celebrated last year the 1,100th anniversary of the Apostle to the Slavs, St. Methodius. In one of those countries Pope John Paul II and other Catholic leaders were invited by the Catholic leadership and ordinary believers of that country to attend the festivities. The government blocked the pope's visit and denied visas for other high-ranking church officials.

Still another Eastern European government allows only organized contacts between church officials subservient to the state and Western church groups and coreligionists. The principal topic of such contacts is not religious issues but publicity for government policies. At the same time that government suppresses independent religious figures who dare to say that the goal of peace requires *both* East and West to rethink their policies. Such individuals are not allowed to leave the country, nor are they given the same opportunity to receive emissaries of religious organizations who visit the state-controlled religious bodies.

We would, nevertheless, be remiss not to recognize progress in the area of increased religious contacts. Recently there have been some fruitful contacts between religious leaders of the Soviet Union and of the United States. Valuable knowledge and spiritual refreshment have been gained from such contacts. But we are concerned that the focus of these contacts is much more narrow than is justified by the letter and the spirit of the Final Act and the Concluding Document. In far too many cases, the dialogue seems to evolve into generalized

115

foreign policy pronouncements delivered by religious officials of the Soviet Union who appear to be little more than spokesmen for their government. How much better would it be for mutual understanding between peoples and faiths if lay activists, local clergy, and ordinary members of the congregations had the opportunity to widen their contacts with, and their understanding of, fellow believers in other parts of the world.

With respect to religious publications and related materials, I must point out that Soviet claims as to the adequacy of these items for believers do not correspond with information we receive from believers themselves. If this were the case, why would so many believers, particularly of the evangelical faith, go to great lengths to obtain Bibles and religious material from abroad or even seek to publish their own? I realize that the Moscow patriarchy of the Russian Orthodox church claims to publish a significant number of Bibles and other religious literature each year, but a large quantity of these items is designated for export abroad or for display in churches and religious sites visited in large part by tourists. Indeed, even a tourist visiting church services—unannounced—at the only officially recognized working Baptist church in Moscow cannot help but notice the paucity of Bibles and song books. The Soviet government maintains that its prohibition on importing Bibles is occasioned by concern that doctrinal errors might be contained in foreign editions. Such concern for the spiritual welfare of its believers might be commendable if it were not out of character with the government's efforts to promote atheism among its citizens, particularly among young people and school students.

Mr. Chairman, in two years the Soviet Union will be celebrating the millennium of the acceptance of Christianity by the peoples of Kievan Rus. The importance of this event to the Slavic peoples of the Soviet Union is indisputable. We hope that the entire world will be able to celebrate this occasion to the fullest and in the most appropriate manner.

Mr. Chairman, I think it is evident that the Soviet Union, however grudgingly, acknowledges the importance that some of its citizens attach to the maintenance of their religious beliefs and ties to co-religionists abroad. It is, therefore, both painful and perplexing to see how Soviet authorities attempt to prevent those of the Jewish faith from learning about their religion, language, and culture and from developing and maintaining contacts with members of their faith in the West. The repressive measures Soviet authorities have taken and are taking are too numerous and substantiated to recount in detail here. But let me mention just a few—they cause puzzlement and dismay.

A Hebrew-Russian dictionary by F. L. Shapiro, published by the Soviets themselves, has been confiscated on numerous occasions from travelers to the USSR. Hebrew translations of works by Yiddish authors Sholem Aleichem and Y. L. Peretz, again both published in the USSR, have also been confiscated. Equally dismaying is the continuing effort of the Soviet authorities to prevent the teaching of the Hebrew language by members of the Jewish community to co-religionists who seek to learn about their religion and cultural roots. Mr. Chairman, I could go on, but I think these examples, as well as those cited by other speakers here, demonstrate the dimensions of the problems faced by those members of the Jewish community who want nothing more than the removal of the special disabilities that plague them so that they can pursue their religious and cultural interests.

Mr. Chairman, the U.S. delegation fully supports BME 26, which aims at only one thing: the implementation of the Helsinki Final Act and Madrid Concluding Document with respect to religious contacts.

23
Right of Reply on Religion

MR. CHAIRMAN: I am glad that the distinguished delegate of the USSR concluded with an appeal to memory. But the memory that has been most present to me, on this Memorial Day of the important victory in Europe of forty-one years ago, goes back a little earlier. On the day when our radio announced the invasion of Poland in 1939, when I was only six years old, I remember my father saying to me—words I didn't quite understand—that what was being announced in Poland was going to be the decisive event of my life. I remember hearing of the Ribbentrop-Molotov agreement. I remember the movement of tanks against Poland, first from Hitler's Nazi Germany on one side, then from Stalin's Soviet Union on the other. The Second World War was a terrible war, and it did cost the awful bloodshed of 50 million lives, as our Soviet colleagues mentioned. But we cannot forget who started it and how it started.

Second, Mr. Chairman, I would like to ask my distinguished colleague from the Soviet Union whether certain words I heard in the English translation actually match the words he used in Russian. These were the exact words used in English: "The one holy subject of the church is peace." Those were the exact words. About these words I have three questions. Is it true that the one subject of the church is peace? Second, are there not other subjects of the historical churches of the Soviet Union, subjects like truth? justice? the examination of conscience? the wrath of a just God? Third, did not church people and many others in 1939 have to learn that there is a difference between "peace" and "appeasement" and that the word "peace" is, therefore, ambiguous? Is the one subject of the church in the Soviet Union peace, or appeasement?

There is one other quotation that I heard in English, and I would ask my distinguished colleague if this is exactly what he meant in Russian. His words in English went exactly as follows: "In the Soviet Union, it is natural for churches to be obedient to government." Are churches in the Soviet Union "obedient to government," and is this taken to be natural? If that is so, it is not what most of us mean by church. It is not what most of us consider the natural relationship between church and government. But it would be important to our understanding to know if what my distinguished colleague said is actually true in the Soviet Union, that the churches are obedient to the government.

There is a further point, Mr. Chairman. I listened intently as my distinguished colleague described freedoms of religion under the Soviet Constitution and other portions of Soviet law. It seemed to me, and I listened to him quite carefully, that the proposal "Bern Meeting of Experts Number 26" corresponds point by point to the provisions of the Constitution of the USSR as our distinguished delegate presented them. [Here Ambassador Novak read through the phrases of BME 26 one by one and asked of each of them whether the right expressed—to make contact with other believers and to communicate with them, to travel, to make pilgrimages, to be in contact through the mails, and so on—were not protected in the Constitution of the USSR. The delegate from the Soviet Union had seemed only moments before to affirm that, one by one, each of these rights is in fact protected in the Soviet Constitution.] This analysis, Mr. Chairman, leads me to ask my distinguished colleague from the Soviet Union a simple question. Does not each provision of BME 26 correspond to a provision of the Constitution of the USSR? And if the Constitution of the USSR does permit each of them, does that mean the Soviet delegation should be permitted to support BME 26? There certainly does not seem to be any conflict between the Constitution of the USSR and BME 26. Have I understood correctly?

Mr. Chairman, a moment ago the distinguished delegate of the USSR said that his delegation opposes BME 26 because it gives privileges to believers but not to atheists. I have read the text of BME 26 quite carefully with that in mind. The text does hold the state to promote those contacts for religious persons that have already been defended in principle in the Helsinki Final Act and the Madrid Concluding Document. If it holds these things for believers, then *a fortiori* it holds them also for atheists. I cannot imagine any of the traditional religions of the Soviet Union depriving atheists of contact with religious believers or religious communities, from making pilgrimages, from acquiring religious objects, and so forth. At the very least, based on the parables of the prodigal son and the lost sheep, religious persons would more than welcome the attendance of unbelievers at religious functions. Quite clearly, the text of BME 26 intends no discrimination whatever, but exactly the reverse.

Finally, Mr. Chairman, the distinguished delegate of the USSR mentioned the rights of Catholics of Lithuania. I wonder if he receives, as I do, each issue of the chronicles of the Catholic church of Lithuania, a record of one of the bloodiest sagas of the acts of the

119

martyrs in a very long time. There have been beatings. There have been murders. There have been imprisonments. There has been commitment to psychiatric hospitals. Lithuania knows again today the blood of martyrs. Thank you very much, Mr. Chairman.

24

On Mail and Postal Interference

MAY 13, 1986

MR. CHAIRMAN: I would like to express our delegation's support for the proposal submitted by the delegations of Turkey and the United Kingdom as BME 17, which recommends that the participating states guarantee the freedom of postal communications in accordance with the universal postal convention, ensure rapid and uninterrupted telephone service in accordance with the international telecommunications convention, and respect the privacy and integrity of all such communications. Such communication is today one of the most fundamental elements of human contacts. The world today is like a village of two or three centuries ago; instant communication keeps even those on opposite sides of the globe in contact. Thus postal and telephone service is a point we should not even have to discuss here, it is so elementary. With regard to mail, the *Guardian* wrote on February 10, 1976:

> The right of private citizens to receive letters through the post may have been thought too elemental for inclusion in the famous Helsinki Final Act. However, the denial of this right is inconsistent with the general principles of free contact and certainly with the spirit of the Final Act.

This right is elementary. We should not have to discuss it, but we do.

Unfortunately, the *Guardian*'s opinion notwithstanding, freedom of the mails is not practiced in all Helsinki states. As many delegations have experienced, a few participating states abridge the clear, international right to send—and to receive—postal communications. There is clear evidence that mail to and from several internationally acclaimed citizens has been tampered with. In 1981–1982, certain emigration invitations were confiscated en masse. Dozens of letters to a famous sculptor from his friends in the West never reached their destination. A photo album of architectural monuments mailed to a priest was returned as "forbidden for entry." In certain cases letters are returned with notations stating that the addressee is not located at the indicated address, when in fact the person has been there all the time. Signed "advice of delivery" forms are returned when letters have not been delivered. In addition, parcel post packages are returned without justification, disappear, or are occasionally delivered with some of the contents missing.

Mr. Chairman, the second aspect of the proposal under consideration is that of telephone communications. All delegations here know that telephone conversations between citizens of some states and interlocutors overseas have been disconnected in the middle of the conversation when certain subjects are raised. Certain private telephones are disconnected, by order of the Ministry of Communications, as "contrary to state interest and public order." During the year 1985 we are aware of at least seventeen such cases. When an independent peace organization solicited ideas for establishing trust between the peoples of East and West, the telephone in their apartment was cut off even though the constitution of that country guarantees the secrecy of postal, telephonic, and telegraphic communications.

Like others in Europe, our many citizens with relatives in a certain country were deeply disappointed at the decision by its authorities in 1982 to discontinue international direct-dialing service. Why was this done? The official reply was "technical reasons." That country is not a backward country in such matters; the mechanical and electronic technologies are available. In technological terms, it appears that direct dialing can be restored at any time to at least the level that had been available before.

Mr. Chairman, who among us—no matter where upon this earth he or she may live—does not wish to hear the voice of a loved one, to receive a letter or gift from a friend, or a photo of a grandchild, or to inquire about the health of relatives in distant lands? And who would in principle deny that right, in any of the political or economic systems in which we live? This is a principle all our nations have supported in the past.

Mr. Chairman, a U.S. senator has asked me to raise another point, which fits within our mandate. Many Ukrainian Americans in Pennsylvania, Illinois, New York, and other states of the United States have tried frantically to make telephonic contact with their relatives near Kiev. Mr. Chairman, if it were possible for the near future, on an emergency basis, to open up special additional telephone lines between the region of Kiev and Ukrainian families around the world, much comfort would be given to many families.

Mr. Chairman, by our acceptance of BME 17, we will strengthen our long-standing commitment, through the Helsinki process, to one of the basic principles of human contacts, the right to communicate freely across borders by post and by telephone. It is fitting that we should do this in Bern, home of one of the original international agreements on these matters. To do so will honor our hosts. And it will bring our peoples a little closer.

25
Remarks on Entry Visas and Exit Visas
MAY 15, 1986

MR. CHAIRMAN: In keeping with our custom of anniversaries, my delegation would like to note that this week we celebrate the tenth anniversary of the founding of Helsinki monitoring groups. My delegation would like to express its personal admiration for those who have suffered so much to further the CSCE process in which we are all engaged, and we would like to express our gratitude to all those others who, while suffering so much, nonetheless work very hard and carefully in monitoring groups in at least seventeen other participating nations. These nongovernmental organizations monitor compliance, examine concepts, and study in advance new developments in the CSCE process and thus are of unusual help to experts such as ourselves.

Mr. Chairman, the main purpose of my intervention today is to discuss the questions of exit visas and entry visas raised by so many delegations, with particular reference to BME 20, 27, 34, and 41. Permit me to begin with a comment by our distinguished delegate and neighbor here at the table, the distinguished delegate from the German Democratic Republic, who spoke yesterday about the need to avoid double standards. Double standards should indeed be avoided. But a double standard occurs when two different standards are used for the same matter, involving terms of an equal character.

The first general point on visas that I would like to make is that exit visas and entry visas are not equal terms. They are asymmetrical. The right of a person to exit from a country is a natural right, protected in the Universal Declaration of Human Rights of the United Nations, whereas entry into a country is not similarly protected in international law. This is a distinction in law and in fact. It follows from common sense. A person cannot be kept against his will in one place. But on the other hand, the same person does not have a similar right to enter into any place at will, because other rights must also be respected. These types of visas, therefore, while related, are not symmetrical and cannot be treated in an identical way. Although from among the numerous proposals before us on the subject of visas, both for entry and for exit, it appears that we might be able to formulate at least one solid proposal in this area, perhaps more. In all such proposals this difference in reality must be respected.

The second general point I would like to make concerns the conditions that affect the issuance of entry visas. We have all agreed that entry visas should be made available in as simple and expeditious a way as possible and should not be subjected to unjustifiable delays. But some of the texts before us speak as if the only reason that might delay the issuance of a visa is procedural. In the real world, this is not the only reason; there are also reasons of volume and potential hidden purposes for entry. Certainly, procedures should be simplified. But this alone will not in all cases make it easy to issue visas immediately.

Population flows around the world are not equal. There are some nations, however small, where the demand for entry, whether as visitors or as immigrants, is very high. There are other nations, whether large or small, where the demand for entry, whether as visitors or as immigrants, is not very large. Countries that show a different volume of requests for visas may experience quite different practical problems in issuing visas. In the United States, for example, even with the help of computers, each year the factor of sheer volume sometimes brings about delays, especially for certain types of visas. Our consular offices issue several thousand visas every day, more than 6 million in a year. This question of volume must be kept in mind.

Third, individual nations often experience a tide of applications for visas made for very different reasons. Sometimes these reasons are disguised. Thus it sometimes happens that a nation may have learned from sad experience that some persons who enter under tourist visas actually intend to take up settlement, whether legally or illegally. Again, some nations may experience that some applicants who come on one sort of visa, perhaps a tourist or a student visa, actually intend to take up illegal work. Again, some nations may experience that certain entrants who come with tourist or student or professional or crew visas actually import dangerous substances like drugs or other socially damaging materials. Again, some nations may experience a flow of entrants who come on a tourist visa or a scientific or cultural or other professional visa but who actually come to take part in a quite different profession, in fact, a profession older than the one usually described as the oldest profession. (In order to find the oldest profession, it was necessary that there be a still earlier profession to tell you where to find it.) Some nations invent new scientific and industrial technologies, and others attempt to capture them. For all these rea-

125

sons some nations learn from experience that they must discriminate carefully among applicants for visas. This is only realistic. We must deal here with the world as it is.

The fourth general point I would like to make is that world population flows are always in fluctuation. Sometimes it happens that the demand for entry into certain nations from other particular nations is very high, while at other times this same demand is relatively low. Thus it was the experience of the United States that the experts were quite wrong in predicting population flows into our country during the 1970s. A very large number of Asian immigrants and visitors entered, much larger than anticipated. At the same time from some Western European countries, for example, the numbers of visitors or immigrants that the experts had anticipated actually fell quite short of projections. Human beings often do not act as the experts predict that they will. Thank God. Human beings freely react to changing circumstances, and thus a realistic visa policy must constantly be subjected to reexamination.

The fifth general point that I would like to make is that the word "entry" must in reality be qualified. In the actual situation of our era, what is covered by that word "entry" actually differs under different social and political systems and in particular countries. In some cases "entry" means that the visitor can talk to other citizens as he or she wills, go where he or she wills, stay where he or she wills. In other countries it may happen that "entry" is quite qualified. A visitor may not talk to citizens of that other country without endangerment; may not enter into the whole country, but only into a very small percentage of it; may not go where he or she wills; may not be free of surveillance in that country; and may not stay where he or she wills. Thus even what we mean by "entry" is, in the real world, not simple and unambiguous. Any proposal we write must reflect these diverse realities.

Finally, and this is perhaps the crucial point, each of the nations of the world is quite different from the others, and any two nations in seeking to erect sensible policies on exit and on entry must necessarily adapt these policies to each other. Thus our government places a strong emphasis upon *bilateral* determinations of such issues. Moreover, our government prefers to conduct these discussions at a much lower and working level, between the appropriate consular offices of the two countries, which are in touch with immediate and concrete realities, rather than in multinational bodies, which necessarily cannot deal with all the attendant complexity and variation. Therefore, any proposal we formulate must reflect the necessary bilateral nature of realistic arrangements.

Mr. Chairman, since a number of nations have expressed an interest in some proposals in this area of exit visas and entry visas, it should not be beyond the capacities of our imagination to draft one or perhaps more proposals that meet the needs of all our participating states and that reflect the complex realities involved. My delegation would be happy to work with all other delegations so interested.

Now for some specific reflections on each of the proposals mentioned above—first on BME 20, submitted by our distinguished colleague from Romania. This proposal calls for the abolition of visas. While the abolition of visas remains something of an ideal for the United States, as exemplified by the open border between our nation and the great nation of Canada, we would not find it possible in the real world as it is simply to abolish visas. The reason is that the lines of persons waiting to get into our country, either as visitors or as immigrants, go around the corner and far into the distance. We are obliged to have a visa system that must be consistent on a worldwide basis, for our consular officers issue visas from 200 posts around the world and at a volume of several thousand every working day, more than 6 million every year. Our experience teaches us that we *must* have a visa system and that it must work in a consistent way for all nations.

Normally, our visa system is open, available, and quick. Many applicants from Western Europe, for example, apply for visas through the mail; the turnaround time is normally shorter than forty-eight hours (to which must be added the time for postal service). For those who apply in person, the visa is normally given in just a few minutes or a few hours, depending upon the length of the line on that particular day. In difficult cases, such as work visas, applicants can discuss their circumstances with professional consular officers in the 200 posts mentioned above.

For first-time applicants from Eastern nations, however, for reasons mentioned above and on the basis of our own experience, our name check procedures may take up to three weeks. Unfortunately, this delay, experience has taught us, is virtually unavoidable.

Proposal BME 27, sponsored by our distinguished colleagues from Bulgaria and the USSR, concerning special visas for workers in the transportation industry, would affect the United States only in the cases of air crews and crews on passenger vessels. We do not yet have bus routes or train routes from Europe to the United States—although I suppose someone somewhere is already working on that. So we would not be so much affected as some other nations. Our visa system already takes these special needs into account. The individual "D" visa for crew members can be issued in a passport or seaman's book. In other cases ship's agents, often while the ship is at sea, submit a crew list to provide group visas for the group. Almost all individual "D" visas are issued for multiple entry.

Perhaps this is a good place to mention the new arrangements made for the special crew visas between Pan Am and Aeroflot on the new routes between New York and Washington and Moscow and Leningrad. Working on a bilateral basis, both sides have agreed to multiple entry visas, provided free and of two years' validity. Our consular offices began immediately issuing these new visas in Moscow. Recently Pan Am informed our government that their Berlin-based crews could not obtain their Soviet visas in Berlin, since Soviet officers in Berlin had not yet been notified of the exact terms of the agreement. But this hitch seems to be being worked out on a smooth bilateral basis. This example shows that bilateral arrangements can often be productive and that progress can be made in the area mentioned by this proposal.

Concerning BME 34, for simplifying the issuance of visas for professional travel, a proposal submitted by our distinguished colleagues from Bulgaria, Czechoslovakia, and the USSR, I must note that our government facilitates visas for professional contacts in the same way as for tourism. In a certain number of cases, prior approval is required from the Immigration and Naturalization Service by our laws. Unfortunately, this petition procedure, though speeded up in recent years, can still take a maximum of several weeks.

Perhaps this is a good point to call attention also to the first tenet of BME 34, which says that the participating states "condemn the practice of placing obstacles in the way of contacts between working people and their professional organizations." We have heard several times from our colleagues in Eastern delegations that the language "placing obstacles in the way of" should be avoided in our proposals. My delegation has no difficulty in using the phrase "placing obstacles in the way of" in those cases in which our implementation review has shown that obstacles have indeed been placed in the way of human contacts. But we would argue that if "placing obstacles" is to be avoided in our proposals, it should also be avoided here. Second, the choice of the verb "condemned," used in this way, sounds to our ear inappropriate for an experts' meeting and for our proposals. Although I must say that "condemned" is a word widely used among theologians, it does not seem to be good CSCE language for an experts' meeting.

Concerning BME 41, a proposal designed to reduce processing time for tourist visas and sponsored by our delegation, I would like to say that the practices of the United States are in the clear on this one. Tourist visas are normally issued very quickly, under the conditions mentioned above. Those who have dealt with our government on visa policy will recognize that our government follows two key policies in this area. The State Department has often expressed its desire to liberalize the issuance of visas and in particular to eliminate fees, to extend validity periods, and to promote multiple entry visas. This makes sense, for our problem is to reduce the volume of material we must handle.

The second principle is reciprocity. Since each nation is different, it is important to deal with these differences on a concrete and realistic level. U.S. policies in this area tend to be reciprocal with the policies of the other state in question. When their fees for various visas are raised, we tend to raise ours, and we tend to apply time limits and other conditions in accordance with their procedures. Because of recent increases in visa fees charged to American citizens by Romania, Czechoslovakia, and Poland, for example, we have recently raised our fees by corresponding amounts. But we would prefer not to do so. We very much favor liberalizing procedures, for obvious reasons, but, like other nations, we do attach a great deal of importance to reciprocity.

In short, if any government of an Eastern European country has a specific proposal on visa schedules, that proposal should be given to our consular officers already in their capitals. That is the level on which such matters should be handled, the working level rather than a policy level. Our policy is to consider such new ideas quickly with a view toward liberalization, if that is at all possible. Here again we favor the bilateral relationship, on a working level basis.

Mr. Chairman, we recognize that one or more proposals in this area may be desired by a number of participating states. We are willing to enter into discussions to construct language that is mutually acceptable and mutually helpful to all our citizens. Thank you, Mr. Chairman.

26
Right of Reply to Poland
MAY 15, 1986

MR. CHAIRMAN: Once again the distinguished delegate of Poland has made a constructive suggestion. I admire the manner in which he commonly proceeds, and welcome him as (I think) a willing member of the new consulting firm of Nowak and Novak. [Laughter] The distinguished delegate from Poland asked two good questions, of considerable practical merit, and to each of them I ought to give a reply.

First, admitting the asymmetry of exit and entry in philosophical terms, he proposed a practical question: When exits from a country exceed entry into another country, what is the practical solution as between those two countries? How can exit be practiced when entry is denied? Two preliminary remarks. Over the centuries Poland has often taken a position of leadership. In the matter of free entry and free exit and a mobile flow of visitations, although my delegation recognizes and has mentioned certain faults in the performance of Poland in recent years, we do admire the extent to which Poland has once again achieved a relatively high degree of openness. It is in the nature of Polish history to do that, and each step forward in these free two-way flows deserves recognition and praise. Second, when Polish citizens come to the United States, they typically make good citizens, and, therefore, typically our citizens welcome them. We have experienced substantial problems, however, with a certain number of Polish citizens coming to the United States on tourist, student, or other visas, only then to use those visas for other purposes than those for which they were issued. This experience has led us to have a higher refusal rate for applications for visas from Poland (in certain categories) than from any other country in Europe. These considerations lead directly to the second question.

That question is: What should be done in practice when flows between two countries are disproportionate and unbalanced, that is, when exit permits for travel in one direction exceed entry permits in the place that those who exit would like to enter? Here we must note that flows between populations change over the years, are often altered, rise and fall. One thing, therefore, is always clear about visa policies: they must always be adjusted to keep pace with changing realities. It often happens that projected flows from one place to another during a coming decade do not in fact materialize, whereas unexpected flows from another place, never predicted by the experts, do materialize. Our delegation, like our government, recognizes the need to place these matters under constant review.

In fact, on the very day when I left the United States for Bern—now it seems so long ago, almost in another life—a front-page article in the *New York Times* (at least, I believe that was the paper I was reading) expressed the dissatisfaction of a large number of American citizens with our current visa policies toward Poland. This is the way in which new problems are often brought to the attention of government officials. In general, we hold that realistic policies must be adjusted to changing conditions. Therefore, I would wish to assure the distinguished delegate from Poland that our delegation stands ready to address changing circumstances, in proposals designed to meet the realities of the moment.

These practical questions by the distinguished delegate from Poland highlight the point I was making earlier: the need for bilateral discussions to deal with questions, such as visas, that are so immediate and practical and vary so much from country to country.

27
Statement on National Minorities and Regional Cultures

by Ambassador Sol Polansky

MAY 16, 1986

MR. CHAIRMAN: On May 7 the distinguished chairman of the Canadian delegation introduced proposal BME 11 on persons belonging to national minorities and regional cultures. My delegation is a cosponsor of that proposal. I would like to speak to that proposal now.

We are a strong and sympathetic supporter of BME 11 because the United States is a country of immigrants. Our historic, religious, ethnic, and cultural heritage has many roots in the regions of all the CSCE participating states, as well as from other regions of the world. Many of our citizens or their ancestors left their former homelands because they were unable freely to pursue their religious, cultural, or political convictions. Had there been a Helsinki Final Act or Madrid Concluding Document then, perhaps the situation would have been better and easier for them. Thus we have great sympathy for those members of national minorities and regional cultures who may have similar concerns today.

Mr. Chairman, just as the United States is a multicultural society, so are many of the countries participating in this Experts' Meeting, and not just from one group or another. Many have national minorities because of migration, the accidents of war, or the moving of borders. All of us assumed solemn commitments under the Helsinki Final Act and the Madrid Concluding Document with respect to national minorities and regional cultures. For example, in the Madrid Concluding Document the participating states stressed the "importance of constant progress in ensuring the respect for and actual enjoyment of the rights of persons belonging to national minorities as well as protecting their legitimate interests." Since many of us have national minorities and regional cultures within our societies, it seems odd that at this meeting there has been only a modest dialogue on this proposal.

Mr. Chairman, in this connection permit me to draw an example from American experience. At the start of World War II, we interned Japanese American citizens in camps because we thought they might be a security risk. This is a part of our recent history of which we are

132

not proud. At the end of the war those American citizens of Japanese ancestry were able to return to their former communities or establish new residences, take up their professions, and renew their family or cultural contacts with relatives and friends in Japan. Those Japanese Americans who felt they had justifiable claims against our government sought and won restitution from the government. They did so through the court system and through Congress. Those same Japanese Americans or their offspring, proud of their heritage and culture, maintain all manner of ties and communications not only with other Americans but also with their families and friends in Japan. Travel in both directions is intensive and normal. Those ties have helped cement close and productive ties between our two nations, only so short a time ago bitter enemies.

At the same time, as we look at what might be termed "CSCE territory," it does not seem to us that there is "constant progress in ensuring the respect for and actual enjoyment of the rights of persons belonging to national minorities or protecting their legitimate interests." Minorities and regional cultures in certain states are still being deprived of the opportunity to maintain family and cultural ties across borders. For example, newspapers in one country have reported artificial delays for visitors at a neighboring country's border crossing points. And we have heard in this hall how one government deprives a minority of important aspects of its ethnic, religious, and cultural identity and heritage. The territories envisaged within the CSCE process are a hodgepodge of ethnic and religious minorities. It has rarely been possible to make geographic boundaries coincide with homogeneous populations. Thus we hear of sufferings and unfulfilled rights.

Mr. Chairman, BME 11 does not seek to create greater rights for members of minorities. It confirms their right to travel for purposes of family reunification, family visits, or personal or professional reasons. These rights are absolute for all citizens whose governments signed the Final Act. BME 11 does, however, seek to ensure that members of minorities should not have any *additional* obstacles placed in their way when they wish to avail themselves of their right to such contacts. Such obstacles, unfortunately, have not been unknown, as our excellent general discussion clearly showed. The constructive dialogue we have had in this phase of our work has encompassed many of the proposals advanced by many delegations. But too little of the dialogue has yet touched on BME 11. We hope the absence of questions signifies a common understanding of its constructive nature. We hope all delegations will accept it. Thank you very much, Mr. Chairman.

28
Remarks on the May 16 Speech by the USSR

MAY 16, 1986

MR. CHAIRMAN: I am grateful to you for permitting my delegation to speak twice this morning, but it did seem wise to comment on the suggestions by the distinguished delegate of the USSR before we enter upon our last free weekend of our time together and before we prepare for the final week of intensive negotiations. My delegation welcomes the clear effort by the distinguished delegate of the Soviet Union to be constructive.

It is an old trick of university professors to say to a new class on opening day, when the students have not yet decided whether to stay in the class for which they are registered, a few words of assurance, such as: "Don't worry, some of you will pass." [Laughter] That is the way all here have necessarily begun to look at our long list of forty-six proposals. It must be clear to all that not all forty-six proposals will pass all our tests.

For its part, our delegation would be quite satisifed to accept all twenty of the Western proposals and perhaps a corresponding number from other delegations, forty in all. [Laughter] I hasten to say that I use the number forty in the high spirit of a Friday session before a weekend. I do want to emphasize, however, that there are many elements among the proposals submitted by Eastern bloc countries that we think deserve consideration in a final document, so that all of us will have a document of real use to the lives of people.

Permit me now a few comments on individual passages in the temperate speech by the distinguished delegate of the Soviet Union. The first of these concerns entry and exit permits. The distinguished delegate of the USSR used the image of a street with one end at one side and another at the other. But this is to take the question of entry visas and exit visas as if they were symmetrical. I argued at some length yesterday, and entirely convinced myself [laughter], that these two types of visas are *not* symmetrical. They are quite different. The right to exit is fully articulated in the Universal Declaration of Human Rights and underlies many of the provisions of the Helsinki Final Act and the Madrid Concluding Document. By contrast, the question of entry envisages many different places of entry and many different possibilities and is not similarly recognized as a right. When a person wants to enter a certain country, his will to enter conflicts with many other rights of citizens of that place and must be considered in that light.

I would suggest to my distinguished colleague from the USSR, therefore, that his metaphor of a single street is much too channeled an image for the reality. I would suggest in its place the image of a home. Surely, a person has the right to exit from that home. If not, others would be justified in thinking of that home as a kind of prison and his position there as a sort of house arrest, in which he was cut off from human contacts of all sorts, kept in exile in a single place. The individual has a right to exit from that home, but that opens not only on a single street but upon the whole wide world, in which there is a very large range of possibilities. Imagine, for example, wanting to visit every town on this planet with a population of at least 25,000. Actually, I once knew a man who had that ambition. The interesting thing about it, he said, is that the world's population and the size of towns keeps changing, so that even when he would complete his visits to all such towns on one continent and then another, new towns kept springing up. So he could continue to pursue his ambition for an entire lifetime. [Laughter] The point is that the questions of exit and of entry are not symmetrical. Any document we produce must recognize that very important difference in reality.

The second question concerns the role of the state. My distinguished colleague pointed out that some delegations here were resistant to the idea of empowering the state; he said this was for "no apparent reason." But there are clear reasons, which many of us have articulated here. In human contacts as in other matters, many of us recognize that the "dead hand" of the state often chills the cheek it touches.

My distinguished colleague from the USSR also said that the role of the state has been "sufficiently defined in the Helsinki Final Act and the Madrid Concluding Document." That is true in the sense required for our immediate purposes; the role of the state *is* spelled out in the Helsinki Final Act and the Madrid Concluding Document. But various delegations have been pointing out here, day after day, the very large domain outside state control, outside state approval, as that domain is defined by the Helsinki Final Act and the Madrid Concluding Document: the role of individual persons who speak for no one but themselves, the role of nongovernmental institutions and nongovernmental organizations and even those associations that individuals freely establish for themselves.

The other day, for example, I cited the section of the Madrid Concluding Document that speaks of free trade unions that persons "freely establish" for themselves. In the view of many of us, the role of the state, as expressed in the Helsinki Final Act and the Madrid Concluding Document, is quite limited. In addition, the realm of agents and actors who act outside the approval of the state is teeming with life, full of energy, and alive with imagination, quite without the control of the state. The objections of many delegations to "statism," that is, to the excessive aggrandizement of the state, absorbing all powers and energies to itself, are well founded in the Helsinki Final Act and the Madrid Concluding Document. These objections are *demanded* by the Helsinki Final Act and the Madrid Concluding Document.

In a later passage the distinguished delegate of the Soviet Union mentioned the "building materials" from the Western proposals that he was prepared to accept and to assemble. In doing so, he mentioned the "Tower of Babylon," that is, the Tower of Babel. That called to my mind another story in the Bible about a tower. It is the parable about how the man who hoped to build a tower must first calculate the number of stones and other resources he had available for this task, lest in building the tower he be embarrassed by mounting only halfway up because he lacked sufficient building materials and other resources. In that case such a man would be obliged to walk away from a monument incomplete for want of sufficient forethought.

My delegation does not believe that the "building materials" assembled by the distinguished delegate of the USSR are yet sufficient for building a tower of which we can all approve. As of today, the distinguished delegate of the USSR probably did not wish to give a comprehensive statement of the building materials he would finally use but only to mention a few of them. We would urge him to reconsider some of the other building materials, which in our view would certainly be necessary to building the kind of tower all of us envisage.

Again, the distinguished delegate of the Soviet Union mentioned certain Western proposals that run "counter" to the Helsinki Final Act. I have carefully reread all the Western proposals, and none of them is designed to run counter to the Helsinki Final Act. On the contrary, every one of them was designed with care and modesty, to use so far as possible the language of the Helsinki Final Act and the Madrid Concluding Document and to contribute to the full and growing design of the CSCE process. This is particularly true when we look at BME 7, on nongovernmental organization, the one proposal that our distinguished colleague singled out in this context.

In our mandate for Bern, we are charged to study "the development of human contacts among persons, individuals and organizations." But any objective reader of the Helsinki Final Act and the Madrid Concluding Document would be obliged to note that when that document speaks of "institutions and organizations" it certainly does not speak only of "*governmental* institutions and organizations." On the contrary, it is often quite explicit about meaning by "institutions and organizations" not only governmental organizations. Clearly and explicitly, the Helsinki Final Act and the Madrid Concluding Document have already accepted *non*governmental organizations.

Let me read the exact words of the first tenet of proposal BME 7: "Remove existing impediments which prevent individuals and the institutions and organizations which they have freely established and joined from maintaining contact, communication and organizational ties with similar organizations in other participating states without need of official sponsorship or approval." Mr. Chairman, the nongovernmental organizations spoken of in this tenet have already been accepted by the Helsinki Final Act and the Madrid Concluding Document. In those documents there certainly is a right for persons freely to establish such nongovernmental organizations and institutions.

Moreover, the Final Act and the Madrid Concluding Document also speak expressly and fully about the rights of human beings in nongovernmental organizations and institutions to establish contact with one another. Clearly, this tenet has in it only such materials as have already been explicitly accepted in the Helsinki Final Act and the Madrid Concluding Document. We would urge our distinguished Soviet colleagues to reread this tenet in that light.

Further, the distinguished delegate of the USSR describes this tenet as a "pretext" for "encouraging illegal and sometimes anticonstitutional activities by all kinds of impostors who speak for no other people except themselves." But BME 7 does nothing of the kind, has not a word about illegal or anticonstitutional activities. Surely, in all participating states, nongovernmental institutions and organizations are both legal and constitutional. In fact, the distinguished delegate expressly points out that "the Soviet delegation certainly does not and cannot have any objection" to "contacts among nongovernmental and public organizations." But that is what the proposal directly and expressly states. So how can the Soviet delegation oppose it?

Mr. Chairman, many of us speaking in private often use the expression "speaking personally." This is an entirely appropriate locution. It is in the nature of free persons that they sometimes speak for no one but themselves. It is a high pleasure to have to represent no one's views but one's own and to speak forthrightly and candidly. It is

137

very good for any country as a whole when each of its many individuals use their intelligence and imagination freely and each says something distinctive that no one else could say. It is the same with institutions. Nongovernmental institutions do not need the approval of the state, and they often speak for no others except themselves. This is not a fault. It is a glory.

Again, the distinguished delegate of the Soviet Union mentioned that some resolutions put forward by NATO are aimed at "undermining the laws and administrative regulations" of certain participating states. But this is true only in the sense already agreed to by those participating states. Through its head of state in the one case, or its foreign minister in the other, each of our participating states did commit itself in the Helsinki Final Act and Madrid Concluding Document to bringing its national laws and administrative regulations into conformity with those two documents. No one here is asking for anything except compliance to commitments already made by each participating state. Far from undermining the commitments of the Helsinki Final Act and the Madrid Concluding Document, all the proposals by the NATO delegations are aimed at making those commitments real in fact.

The next point, Mr. Chairman, is a little delicate to treat of. Each increment of travel by citizens of the USSR, for family visits and family reunification, as outlined by the distinguished delegate of the USSR in his remarks, is much appreciated. Every time a person is allowed to visit his family, or a family is permitted to be reunited, one of the most penetrating pleasures of human life is achieved: the pleasure of being with one's own family. So in every single case such travel is much welcomed, and the numbers cited by the distinguished delegate of the USSR are to be praised. Still, it must be pointed out, if even 1 percent of the population of the USSR made such a visit once a year, that would be a total of 2.7 milion visits. That is a number far in excess of the 110,000 Soviet citizens who traveled to CSCE participating states for various family reasons during 1985, as cited by our distinguished colleague. Even a half of 1 percent of all Soviet citizens would be 1.35 million, not 110,000. The tone of voice of the distinguished delegate of the USSR suggested that in citing figures he was hoping that the numbers would increase in the future and that he was not entirely satisfied with the numbers of the recent past.

This brings me to one of the most important sentences in his intervention. I have been waiting for such a sentence all through our proceedings, as a stretch of sand awaits a rain. Our distinguished colleague said on page 7: "It is quite possible that the *practice* which exists in our country with regard to these matters may also leave room for improvement" (emphasis added). No doubt, Mr. Chairman, this is a sentence that each of our delegations, in varying degrees, could assert. It is a welcome sign of that self-criticism, that openness, that transparency, that General Secretary Gorbachev has called for and that is so essential to the growth of compliance with CSCE commitments. I was very happy to hear that sentence.

Finally, Mr. Chairman, I was sorry that the distinguished delegate of the USSR added his final paragraph, about the speech given the other evening by the general secretary of the Communist party of the Soviet Union, on a subject outside our mandate. To be sure, this was a very short paragraph, compared with the long, constructive remarks that preceded it. Still, I was very sorry that the distinguished delegate of the USSR did not resist the impulse to include it. For it presents my delegation with two delicate problems. First, here in this room, that paragraph on a subject not connected to our mandate injected a touch of propaganda, just at the moment when we are beginning an important negotiation of our own. Second, the speech of the general secretary was itself received by my delegation as facing in each of two directions. One face pointed toward genuine negotiations, and the other pointed toward rather harsh criticism of the United States and to propaganda. Mr. Chairman, it is necessary for me to say that one can have *either* serious negotiations *or* propaganda. One cannot have both.

Mr. Chairman, our delegation, like our government, will choose to listen to the voice expressing a desire for serious negotiations, not to the voice suggesting propaganda. In this way we hope to contribute to building the sort of realistic progress that each delegation here will be proud to report to the world, without fear of its being laughed at for its excessive modesty. Thank you, Mr. Chairman.

29
Monitoring Compliance with the Helsinki Final Act: Draft of Plenary Address

MAY 14, 1986

MR. CHAIRMAN: In speaking in favor of BME 7, encouraging human contacts among nongovernmental organizations, my delegation barely mentioned the responsibilities the work of the CSCE process has imposed upon the citizens of Europe and North America. The Helsinki Final Act, and even more the Madrid Concluding Document, spoke eloquently of the human rights of individuals and their free associations. It also spoke of their duties and responsibilities.

Each person has dignity in only one way: by taking responsibility. Merely to conform, or to shirk personal responsibility, is to fail in humanity. Thus the authors of the Helsinki Final Act had every reason to know that, all around the world, noble men and women would win their dignity by accepting responsibility for the realization of the Helsinki Final Act. They would monitor compliance.

What are words without actions? Only air. The Helsinki Final Act was intended to change reality, not merely to riffle air.

No government—and certainly no ruling elite—is objective enough to monitor its own compliance. For this, only independent bodies of well-informed citizens can be effective. Human rights, James Madison once said (and the same holds true for rights to human contacts), are defended not by "parchment barriers" but only by free associations of individuals, whose moral habits give them vigilance and courage. Citizens must act together to ensure the protection of their rights, or there are no rights.

In virtually every participating state, therefore, citizen monitoring groups spontaneously grew up, nourished by the Helsinki Final Act. They grew up in America, in Western Europe, in Eastern Europe, and

---

This text was not actually delivered in plenary. A copy of it was shared with the heads of principal delegations, particularly with the head of the delegation of the USSR, for transmission to Moscow.

in the Soviet Union. This week, in fact, we celebrate the tenth anniversary of their founding. Ten years later one of the saddest chapters of the CSCE process has been the imprisonment by certain governments of these brave monitors. Here in Bern we experts are well housed, well fed, well feted, while others of our fellows in this CSCE process, no less serious—perhaps even more so—now suffer from excruciating injections in psychiatric hospitals or are ill and badly fed and worked to exhaustion in labor camps. Some have died from their mistreatment. These brave ones, never to be forgotten in the golden annals of just men and just women, will one day be the glories of the world and of the nations of their birth. Today we all remember them and recall their names, one by one, in honor. They come from many countries. They represent Helsinki monitoring chapters, Amnesty International, Charter 77, and Vons.

Besides these, Mr. Chairman, there are others who, while they do not suffer, nonetheless work with devotion and for long hours, trying to be certain that this noble CSCE process comes to some real effect. In this category, Mr. Chairman, are many monitors in many countries. But since our meeting in Bern has come to a point at which all of us are working toward a closing document, I thought it might be useful to share with you a useful checklist prepared by one such group. The distinguished nongovernmental organization Helsinki Watch, with offices in New York and Washington, a founding member of the International Helsinki Federation for Human Rights, has prepared several ideal proposals by which to judge the real proposals of the Bern Meeting of Human Experts. Helsinki Watch is led by such distinguished citizens as Robert Bernstein, Orville Schell, Norman Lear, Sol S. Chaikin, Robert Penn Warren, Jerome Wiesner, Liv Ullmann, Arthur Miller, and many others.

These proposals, Mr. Chairman, bear recalling as we enter our final ten days. I think we can be proud that in our meeting so far we have discussed virtually all of them. I quote now from those that relate to principles and procedures—our present subject—not to individual cases, which we are discussing bilaterally.

• Affirm the principle of the Helsinki Final Act that citizens must be guaranteed the right to "know and act upon their rights."
• Release from prison, labor camp, exile, and psychiatric confinement the forty-nine men and women who were members of the citizens' Helsinki monitoring groups and their affiliates. Of particular concern are the cases of Dr. Yuri Orlov, chairman of the Moscow Helsinki group; Dr. Anatoly Koryagin, member of the psychiatric commission; Mykola Rudenko, chairman of the Ukrainian Helsinki

group; and Viktoras Petkus, member of the Lithuanian Helsinki group, all of whom are in poor health and have suffered from mistreatment and extremely harsh conditions.

• Return Dr. Andrei Sakharov to his Moscow residence and permit him to resume a normal life there with his wife, Yelena Bonner, ensuring that they are allowed unhindered contact with their relatives and colleagues in the Soviet Union and abroad.

• Resolve cases of divided families by facilitation of emigration applications. Permit reapplication in a timely manner, and supply detailed documentation on the grounds for refusal of emigration permits. Cease harassment, intimidation, detention of families who have sought to emigrate to join relatives abroad. Facilitate binational marriages and process applications to join spouses quickly.

• Allow regular visits between family members residing in different countries. Process applications for temporary visits speedily. Provide documentation for the grounds of refusal of visas in a timely manner, with a mechanism for appeal and rapid reapplication. Particular attention must be shown to quickly handling requests for visits in medical emergencies, or to attend the funerals of relatives.

• Permit travel abroad for reasons of medical care at the applicant's discretion upon invitation from either individual foreigners or foreign medical institutions, without demanding approval from the home country's ministries of health or other agencies, and regardless of the type of equivalent medical care that may be available in the applicant's home country. Permit foreign physicians to visit their patients in their home countries without interference. Permit unhindered mailing or delivery of medicines that are recognized or authorized for production by the government of the patient's home country, but which may be in short supply or prohibitively expensive in the home country.

• Facilitate granting of visas for business or personal travel. Ease requirements for exchange of a certain amount of currency per day and restrictions on the amount of foreign currency that may be purchased. Provide complete explanations for reasons of refusal in a speedy fashion.

• Explore avenues for facilitating and subsidizing tourism between participating states. Repeal existing laws that require citizens to report on any contacts with foreigners to local authorities. Repeal existing Soviet law stipulating fines of citizens who provide transportation or lodging to foreigners without prior notification of local officials. Initiate procedures to permit foreign tourists to board in private homes or with friends and relatives, rather than requiring that foreigners stay only in state hotels. Increase the length of time permitted for tourist trips. Provide complete explanations for refusal of tourist visas and cease the practice of denying visas without cause or not responding in any way to applications for visas, thus disrupting travel plans. Cease the practice of having security agents follow tourists or use electronic surveillance to monitor their movements.

• Cease interference with mail and telephone communication. Establish direct-dialing telephone calling and permit collect calls or person-to-person calls to be made to contacts abroad. Permit the use of automatic answering devices. Cease the practice of interrupting international phone calls or shutting off caller's phone service because of international phone calls. Provide detailed explanation for non-delivery of mail and packages. Ensure that mail sent with a registered receipt to be signed only by the addressee reaches the addressee, and that the addressee's reply postcard is returned to the sender. Ease heavy duty fees on packages sent from abroad, and reestablish the practice of permitting the sender to pay all duty and postage fees on behalf of the recipient at the point of mailing.

• Permit the delivery of invitations to attend international conferences, events, academic exchanges, etc., either through the regular mails, or by representatives of foreign embassies of the senders. Process in a timely manner applications to attend international conferences upon invitation or at the discretion of the applicant. Supply full documentation on grounds for refusal.

• Facilitate travel for contact between coreligionists, to attend religious ceremonies or conferences. Allow mailing or hand delivery of religious literature and articles between states without interference by customs agents or local authorities. Increase opportunities, now very restricted, for religious believers to study in seminaries abroad, or for clergy to carry out missionary work in the country.

• Increase opportunities for youth of participating countries to travel or study abroad, including residence in private homes, and to meet with each other without interference during international conferences or events.

• Permit unhindered access to foreign embassies in the participating states. Cease the practice of discouraging entry to foreign embassies through intimidation, surveillance, or detention.

Mr. Chairman, the expectations that responsible citizens have for the CSCE process are immense. Still, we can take some satisfaction. Many of the proposals already tabled here at Bern meet at least some of these expectations. Nonetheless, our citizens—and history itself—hold us to very high standards. In many ways, thoughtful citizens are ahead of governments, pressing governments to do ever more to advance security and mutual cooperation. But this is exactly what the

Helsinki Final Act keeps insisting upon—greater improvement, constant development, further advance—not in the world of abstract ideals, but in that real world inhabited by ordinary citizens.

Thomas Jefferson once said: "The care of human life and happiness, and not their destruction, is the first and only legitimate object of good government." It is in this light that the monitors around the world are watching us. Their standards seem high, in the lenses of government, but not at all high in the lenses of citizens who value "the care of human life and happiness." Open contact with loved ones gives the most penetrating happiness to human beings. The Helsinki Final Act commands us to take care of that.

In our last ten days, Mr. Chairman, we must set our standards high. We must do the best that realists can to take steps that unmistakably bring the world closer to compliance with the Helsinki Final Act. We, too, are monitors.

30
Sakharov's Birthday
MAY 21, 1986

[The first six paragraphs below were delivered extempore in response to remarks by the delegate of the USSR.]

MR. CHAIRMAN: The distinguished delegate of the Soviet Union just used two key words on which I wish to elaborate in my remarks: He mentioned realism—the subject on which I intended to speak. He also mentioned the word "gloom." It is one of the advantages of having one's grandparents come from Central Europe, whose political history is full of so much pain, that the *normal* world is thought to be gloomy. In fact, one is happy only when one is gloomy. When things are going badly, the world seems normal, one feels secure and without illusions. When things are going well, one thinks they must be kidding you.

In certain ways pessimism is a very good basis for dealing with reality; there is certainly a lot of evidence in favor of it. But the best part about basing one's capacities for action on pessimism is that one is constantly surprised by every good thing that happens. One expects the worst and is able to carry on in face of the worst. That is why we say, in the United States, that certain athletes of Central European background make excellent quarterbacks. When their team is down 20–7 with only several minutes to play, they think, "What's new?", lower their heads, and play football. That turns out to be a very good way to play the game and often results in last-minute victory.

Thus, Mr. Chairman, although I did not intend to comment at all upon our discussions in the sounding group yesterday, the comments by the distinguished delegate of the USSR oblige me now to do so. It is important that everyone recognize how terribly pessimistic the Western delegations felt on learning the news from those soundings.

The distinguished delegate of the Soviet Union said today that 70 percent of the Western proposals were acceptable to him, with a few changes of a word here or there. That would mean fourteen of our twenty proposals. Actually, Mr. Chairman, we learned in the sounding group that of our twenty modest and carefully constructed proposals, meant to deal with specific problems, eight were rejected out of hand as nonnegotiable, and at least eight others were subject to crippling amendments. These amendments would frustrate any good the proposals were designed to do and would prevent them from dealing with the problems they were aimed at correcting.

So it is true that the news we heard from the Warsaw Pact nations inspired in us a great sense of depression, gloom, pessimism. But for me at least, gloom is only normal. There is nothing to be disturbed about. We are certain that the Soviet Union and its allies were simply setting forth before us, at that stage, the difficulties they had found in our proposals and offered the information that we, in turn, were seeking. The Warsaw Pact countries have not yet set forth their beginning negotiating position. So we will get on with our work with a sense of realism and a sense of hope. So much for gloom.

The word "realism," Mr. Chairman, brings me to my second point. It is one thing to speak about negotiations on proposals, and it is another to confront the realities of real lives in the real world and the situation of human contacts among actual persons in our time. Let me mention one such person.

One of the great Russian citizens of our time, three-time winner of the Lenin Prize, a humanist held in immense international esteem as a physicist, a recognized genius, a citizen whose human contacts are today extremely limited, is today celebrating his sixty-fifth birthday in a city far from home and family. My delegation would like to extend its deepest respects to Dr. Andrei Sakharov, whose situation in so many ways invites us to reflect upon the development of human contacts in our time.

How this great man would benefit by human contacts! He might be lecturing, traveling, leading seminars. And many in the world would benefit immensely by contacts with him.

Mr. Chairman, these reflections lead me to my third point. There should be no gap between concentration upon negotiating on our proposals and attending to realities. For three weeks we did discuss real problems. And again for the next two weeks we also described the real problems that our new proposals are intended to alleviate. This is particularly true of each of the twenty carefully drawn Western proposals. Each has been designed to meet a specific problem that experience since Helsinki has forced upon our attention. We must keep such realities in mind as we look at our proposals and the proposed amendments to them. How will our final proposals—our legacy—actually affect reality?

With this question in mind, Mr. Chairman, I recently reread a checklist of realities that I brought with me to Bern—a checklist of realities this conference ought to address. This list is very comforting, Mr. Chairman. We did discuss almost all the items on it. It helps to show how good our discussion has been. It also helps to show how good our final list of proposals yet must be.

I quote from a list of questions sent me by a group of distinguished Americans, some of whom I am proud to count as friends, who wished to assist me in my work. I quote from the sections of their letter that bear most upon matters related to the proposals now before us. [Ambassador Novak read here the detailed checklist supplied by Helsinki Watch, from the undelivered text of May 14, above.]

Mr. Chairman, many of our delegations must have such lists. It is of some considerable comfort to see that we *have* managed to discuss virtually all these points during our debates. Some of our discussions were hard and deep indeed.

Now we must show realism. Our aim, after all, is to help real people. We must keep their faces in mind as we approach the final decisions on the proposals now before us.

31
Words versus Compliance: Concluding Plenary Address

MAY 27, 1986

MR. CHAIRMAN: For ten and a half years now, the Helsinki process has sought to improve the lives of ordinary people. In many respects it has succeeded. Human contacts are in several states freer and more open than they were ten years ago. This is a precious gain.

Alas, in other states human contacts are in some respects worse.

Beginning eight weeks ago, all of us assembled here pledged that we would examine those matters unblinkingly and without illusions. And so we did.

At Bern my delegation discerns three significant achievements. First, there were the individual persons helped, if not always precisely *because* of Bern, nonetheless *occasioned* by our meeting here. We do not have a precise count of the persons—but do know that they number nearly a thousand—earlier not permitted to be reunited with their spouses or children who, because Bern took place, have the promise to be in the company of their loved ones.

It was worth it, during these hard weeks in Bern, to play a small role in a process that actually helped so many persons. Would that there had been thousands more!

Second, we had at Bern a penetrating review of compliance and performance. Anyone who reads the Helsinki Final Act and the Madrid Concluding Document feels immediately in the presence of truly noble documents. They have a visionary power. Yet the real need at this point in history is not so much for new documents as for compliance with existing documents. The test for the Helsinki process is not the producing of new documents. The test is compliance and performance.

Our debates here were honest; the spirit was candid. We argued mightily with one another. We showed clearly, over and over, those places, those practices, and those methods by which the noble ideals of Helsinki and Madrid, affirmed on paper, are frustrated in daily reality. Our implementation review was one of the best, veterans of past meetings have said, in CSCE history. We heard countless suffer-

148

ings described. We heard how millions are separated from human contacts elsewhere considered normal. We heard many voices of pain. Our mail bags brought us new materials every day. There are fewer excuses for illusions than there were eight weeks ago.

The third great success of the Bern meeting lay in an incremental growth of a common European language, the ancient language of our hearts and intellects, our ideals and hopes. More and more, the debates of CSCE create a common body of thought for all of Europe, a European conscience.

These are three great gains: individual persons helped; a clear-eyed examination of reality, without illusions; and the slow raising of international standards, according to a new common moral language.

Mr. Chairman, all these gains depend on words. Words inspire them. Words guide them. But in the end only those words have weight that embed themselves in reality, that are complied with and put into performance. The words of this Helsinki process are especially precious, but also especially fragile. They have highest value when they are complied with. They gain their weight from performance.

Many delegations among us repeated that free and open contacts among persons have deteriorated in recent years in certain vivid ways: divided spouses, disunited families. Compliance has declined. In such circumstances precious words lose meaning.

The strength of the founding documents of this process depends upon the credibility of words. That is why, to even the scales of the demonstrated decline in compliance in recent years, my government knew that a Bern document would have to set a high standard. Otherwise the public would lose confidence. And confidence building is the essence of the Helsinki process.

Every delegation here knows the brilliant and careful work of the coordinators from the neutral and nonaligned delegations. They fairly reflected the long, slow course of our negotiations. They performed at the highest human level.

But our CSCE process works, rightly, through consensus. Each step in our negotiations, rightly, demanded compromise. In order to achieve compromise, as is normal, loopholes creep into the text. To the right to travel, for example, was added the loophole "when personal and professional circumstances permit." Honest authorities will understand this one way, but cynical authorities will use it to alter such circumstances at will. Loopholes are sometimes necessary. But, cumulatively, they eat like moths into our founding documents. Inevitably, too, robust proposals lost weight. Until the end it was impossible to add up the weight of all together. When at last my government could weigh them, it found the document too thin, containing loopholes damaging to compliance.

My government takes words seriously. In our country, there is uneasiness about the growing gap in the Helsinki process between words and compliance. A document reduced in weight by many compromises, it judged, would injure the process all of us cherish and must protect.

Mr. Chairman, my delegation deeply respects all our colleagues in this room, with whom we worked so hard and long. We are deeply grateful to our Swiss hosts. We believe that the CSCE process gains in strength from paying strict attention to the connection between words and compliance. Our government looks forward eagerly to resuming the long, patient, and crucial work of this process in Vienna.

The debates at Bern have paved the way for Vienna. In compliance and performance, work to improve human contacts will speed up. Bern has given an undeniable impetus to basic issues of human contacts. Bern has launched a new seriousness about compliance—and it has underlined the extreme seriousness of fundamental words. This is its historic legacy.

Deepest thanks are due to the government of Switzerland for making this good meeting possible.

PART THREE
The Aftermath

32
The Endgame

I had gone to bed at about 5 A.M. Monday, May 26, supposedly the day of final formalities, after the Soviets had walked out of our negotiations at 4 A.M. It seemed then that the issue of a final document was dead. I felt relief. No more decisions would be necessary. We had tried hard for a good document. Neither the Helsinki Commission of the Congress nor the State Department wanted us to sign a poor document. Meanwhile, the review of compliance had been excellent and, in several of the Eastern European states, if not in the USSR, many concrete cases had been favorably resolved. Our main goals in Bern had been achieved.

I had to be back at work two hours later, shortly after 7 A.M., for a congressional breakfast and a talk introducing a television documentary on the divided spouses in Moscow. Afterwards, at 9:30 A.M., I was suddenly surprised by a last-ditch, take-it-or-leave-it compromise document worked out by the Neutrals and the Nonaligned (N-plus-N). It embraced the much-weakened batch of proposals tentatively agreed upon before negotiations broke down at 4 A.M. But it dropped the most controverted ones (the ones most important to us). It accepted the last Soviet version of the proposal on religious liberty (omitting mention of rights of persons). It also contained a Soviet reference excluding migration to Israel from the proposal on national minorities. This proposal was especially important to Canada, Yugoslavia, and the United States, among others. We had energetically rejected the reference to Israel the night before—it was astonishing to find it still present. When this was pointed out to them, the representatives of the N-plus-N were embarrassed to find that they had retained it. They solved the problem simply by omitting the whole proposal. This greatly pleased the Soviets, who abhorred any mention of "national minorities."

My heart sank as I looked over the compromise document. At the meeting of the western caucus, I said I would need to consult with Washington before accepting it and was extremely pessimistic. But Germany was most eager to accept and had so persuaded the caucus of the European Community (the EC12) in their earlier meeting. Time pressures were immense because the whole meeting was supposed to end this day with formal statements. Reluctantly, most of the others were prepared to accept the N-plus-N compromise as the best we could get. It did not meet my criteria, but by now the emotional groundswell in favor of accepting it was almost universal. (I came to see the hard way that documents should *never* be expected from meetings whose time frame has been fixed in advance. Agreements should never be rushed into. "The best we can get" is not equivalent to "good enough.")

It was clear that, although a formal vote would not be taken, most delegations were now reluctant to stand up and publicly dissent. Besides ourselves, only a few needed to telephone their capitals for final approval. For most, this entailed a call within the same time zone, to offices already open. By the time we could reach Washington, where it was at that time not yet 3 A.M. in the middle of a long holiday weekend, all others would probably be bowing to the political groundswell. I still hoped that others also might block consensus; one or two were reluctant. But I began to fear that the United States would stand alone, given the long delay we would face in reaching Washington.

By noon, however, I had reached both the assistant secretary of state for European affairs, Rozanne Ridgway, and the assistant secretary for human rights, Richard Schifter. Once they heard the final wording of the proposed compromise document, the two assistant secretaries of state most responsible judged immediately that we should say no. Both agreed that the document was unacceptable. That relieved me greatly, even though I dreaded having to carry that word to others. I signaled this word to Ambassador Torovski, who was leading the "contact group" for the N-plus-N.

I had tried very hard to achieve what had not been achieved in Ottawa or in Budapest, a good step forward, codified in a good final document. I had thought that Bern could be a turning point in "openness." And at the moment, we seemed to have failed.

At about 2 P.M., I was summoned to receive an urgent cable from our embassy in Moscow. It recounted how our consular officers there had been summoned to the Foreign Ministry at 9 A.M. and then told to come back two hours later. When they did so, they were made to wait. Then they were handed a list of thirty-six families that had been given permission to leave, with a pledge that thirty-six others would be given similar permission very soon. Some families well known to the embassy were on the list. Here at last, perhaps, were the "concrete cases," the "concrete results," we had waited for in vain since our trip to Moscow ten weeks earlier.

Sadly, though, these lists came too late to change our decision in Bern. We had twice earlier been given long lists by Ambassador Kashlev in Bern, and on both occasions the permissions given had been routine and did not reflect new movement. To agree to a document because of movement on concrete cases would have set a bad precedent for future negotiations. It would be like trading agreements for hostages.

Because we could not verify the lists released in Moscow, I said nothing about them publicly in Bern and neither did Ambassador Kashlev.

The great joy I felt that seventy-two families were being released in Moscow was tempered by two nagging fears. The first was that this would be another false alarm, merely routine releases, having nothing to do with our long lists of especially aggrieved persons. The second was that, since we had already decided to reject the Bern compromise document, the Soviets would retaliate by withdrawing these cases. That would be very sad.

Meanwhile, my duty was to telephone Washington with the news and to inform Ambassador Torovski of the new development. The Germans and the EC12 had urged Torovski and me to keep the decision open until their foreign ministers could consult directly with Secretary Shultz. I said that no change was likely but that we would give them a chance to appeal. Some in our delegation thought that the "concrete results"—seventy-two cases, an unprecedented number— justified a different decision. I did not. But Washington had other issues to consider, and that decision would be theirs. Assistant Secretaries Ridgway and Schifter agreed with me.

By now Washington had the Bern document in hand by cable, as well as the Moscow cable. Secretary of State Shultz was reached in Washington by Foreign Minister Genscher from Ankara, Turkey, where he was on a state visit. After asking for a review, the secretary held firm and so informed the German foreign minister.

The day was a long one. For almost twelve hours, we waited for these consultations to be concluded. It seemed like a month.

It was my painful task to announce at the much-delayed plenary session just before 9 P.M. (what a long day it had become, after two hours' sleep) that the United States must withhold its consent. Having weighed it, I said, we found it a weak document, given the pattern of noncompliance with existing documents so amply documented during our discussions at Bern. Since in the excitement of the last hours everyone becomes driven by the need to bring forth a document, my announcement was greeted with almost universal disappointment. That disappointment was all the more acute because of prior failures to agree upon a document at earlier experts' meetings in Ottawa and Budapest during the preceding year. At Bern, the United States had clearly led the way in trying very hard to get an agreement this time. At one level, then, my mood was heavy and sad.

At another level, nonetheless, I felt honored to bring forward a clear, unstampeded, reasoned rejection of a weak document. I had dreaded the thought that, in the future, loopholes introduced by the Bern proposals might be used to deny good human beings their natural rights to emigrate or to visit as they chose, that Bern would make things worse rather than better.

It is not so easy to be almost isolated and to stand alone. At such times, one is nourished by a quiet part of the soul that clings to a judgment about what is right, on the merits, apart from outside pressures. I was simultaneously very troubled in Bern and quietly very happy.

After the announcement of our decision, I went immediately to a large, packed press conference. It was about 9:30 P.M. The lights were bright. I appreciated the fact that Congressman Steny Hoyer, there with the Helsinki Commission, came and stood near me. I explained the U.S. decision calmly and clearly, fighting back the exhaustion brought on by lack of sleep. Our case was a strong one: the larger pattern of noncompliance with the existing agreements and our unwillingness in this context to accept what even its staunchest admirers described as a modest, weak step. In the field of human rights and human contacts, I said, words matter. They receive their historical meaning only from deeds. The United States would not assent to words unlikely to be backed up by deeds. Indeed, some of these words were likely to be used to justify certain patterns of abuse. We would look forward to a stronger, better draft in Vienna.

The final closing speeches began at 10 P.M. and recessed at midnight until the next morning. During them, I had to compose my own closing speech. Press copies and copies for the translator would need to be typed by delivery time the next morning. The entire meeting would run over into the next day, causing great havoc to the plans of the hotel and all departing participants.

That night I had nightmares about the probable reaction to this bold dissent. Perhaps everyone in the United States would consider it a failure. The European press was likely to be very hostile; blaming Americans is a habit well-entrenched in many circles. I was very distressed that I had not planned the ending better. Worst of all, I feared that, despite all my hopes for greater openness in the USSR, the anger expressed by the Soviet delegation in Bern would be echoed by a greater rigidity in Moscow, making the lot of dissidents and refuseniks worse. My hope was that our seriousness in Bern would, on the contrary, be a salutary shock. But I could not know then whether such hope was illusory. I had a horrible night.

My scheduled trip to Portugal for a lecture to coincide with the publication of *The Spirit of Democratic Capitalism* in a new Portuguese translation had to be canceled.

Instead of traveling to Lisbon the next morning, I gave my closing speech. Torovski, who sat next to me, attacked it severely in his turn. Coming from a friend, that was a blow. Eickhoff could barely suppress his desolation and his rage. Still, most of the delegations spoke of the larger issues of noncompliance and the necessity of stronger agreements in Vienna. The Yugoslav mocked my earlier words about "ordinary people"—the most frequently used phrase at the conference—and said that "ordinary people" would suffer because of our denial of consensus. Kashlev boasted about "the new spirit" in the USSR and the "old spirit" in the United States and tried to picture the United States (and Canada) as "far away," across the ocean from "Europeans" (including the Soviets, of course). I had, in one sense, given Moscow an easy propaganda victory.

But not really. From all around the world I was to receive support from those who take the Helsinki process seriously, who cherish its hard-won words, and who do not want to see them emptied of reality. The announcement by Moscow that seventy-two families would be released gave the world a vivid picture of "concrete results" at Bern and reminded the world of other millions struggling for elementary liberties. Several Western European delegations took pains to tell me privately that they were glad not to be saddled with the Bern document.

Criticism by the press and others on the scene in Bern was, to say the least, very intense. True, a significant number of Western delegates agreed with our decision and were glad that we had made it. The Germans, of course, felt crushed. Ambassador Eickhoff—my good friend, with whom I had become so close, his room being down the hall from mine, and for whose sake I had done so many things to promote issues dear to him—was ashen-faced with despair. A few lines in the final agreement affecting human contacts between West and East Germany were especially important to Eickhoff, and nothing pained me more than to see those lines lost with the others. In actual fact, these points were covered by the Helsinki Final Document, but the Germans had wanted them reasserted in a particular way.

The Swiss, our hosts, and the Austrians who worked with them in the Neutrals-plus-Nonaligned caucus were extremely disappointed, even angry. It was, after all, their compromise that we rejected. The Soviet delegation was visibly upset, surprised by our final no, and worried about the final gambit that Moscow had played. They attacked the United States acidly in their continuing comments to the press.

In the United States, most commentators seemed pleased that their government had not gone along with a bad agreement. Even those who criticized our rejection of the compromise document could find little in it actually to praise.

Senator Malcolm Wallop, one of the key senators in the Helsinki Commission, sent me a glowing letter, in the name of those who had been skeptical of the Helsinki meetings, thinking them a charade. He was delighted to see important words taken seriously. Among many such, the effect was bracing.

As I had hoped during the hours of exhaustion and concern, a great many of the persons whose judgments I most admired welcomed this decision. But there were also critics.

A typical criticism was launched against me on my return to the United States by an old friend, Leonard Sussman, executive director of Freedom House. Leonard had just published a small book of mine on human rights. Like him, I thought of myself as a realist; we both opposed utopianism. But Leonard's judgment in particular cases was sometimes softer than mine. For example, we had been on opposite sides on another recent issue, the withdrawal of the United States from UNESCO, which I supported and Leonard had resisted. In this case, Leonard came down pretty hard on me in testimony before the Helsinki Commission of the Congress. He said how confused he was by reading on the same day adjacent columns in his newspaper, one dispatch from Moscow reporting the release of seventy-two families and one from Bern saying that the United States in isolation had said "no" to a document that everyone else supported. "At that moment," he said, "the Soviets had arranged to release 117 citizens for reunion with families in the United States—the largest such reunion on record. That was the moment we chose to kill a statement favoring incremental improvement in human contacts—hardly the appropriate carrot for the direct Soviet act of complying even minimally with earlier commitments."

Sussman could not know and did not present the actual sequence of events accurately. Our dissent had come first, the news of the release second. I was thoroughly delighted to have Leonard observe that I had helped to achieve "the largest such reunion on record." The Soviets had, in fact, used our delegation as the focal point for the release of a larger number of persons than they had seen fit to release for President Reagan in Geneva the preceding November. Since I had raised the question of concrete cases incessantly, and with a broad range of fresh arguments, beginning at the Foreign Ministry in Moscow in March, this outcome pleased me greatly. The document, alas, was another matter and had to be judged on its own terms.

Sussman argued, further, that *all* documents in the Helsinki process are flawed by compromises, loopholes, and ambiguities. This is inherent in the procedure of consensus. (In the Helsinki process no votes are actually taken; to block consensus, a delegation need only speak up.) Thus, Sussman judged that the compromise final document represented at least some forward movement, not much, but enough for those who believe in patience and gradualism. Sussman also expressed fears that the United States seemed to be backing out of the Helsinki process altogether.

Sussman had this last point exactly backwards. Far from backing out of the Helsinki process, the United States believed that it was necessary to *rescue* it, to restore its credibility, to show that it is strong enough so that the United States can say *no* as well as *yes*, and not just automatically be dragged along. Further, Sussman's lecture on patience was singularly inappropriate. Our delegation had just eaten full plates of patience for eight concentrated weeks and had gone round the clock more than once trying to gain a substantive result.

Sussman's critique boiled down to his judgment that the compromise document marked some small advance beyond Helsinki and Madrid. I had heard that issue argued both ways and formed a judgment opposite to his. True, one could stress the tiny gains made in some of the Bern proposals. But one should also count the tiny losses—the razor slashes of a dozen cuts at crucial places. A final judgment on the issue cannot be black or white. One has to look at the document as a whole, shake it, and weigh it.

In Bern, it would have been a delight to have found the compromise adequate. But to defend its actual words in the presence of those already most cynical about the process seemed to me unacceptable. The Bern compromise would have cost the Soviets virtually nothing. It contained very little that the Western nations had asked for, and it created some new loopholes that might prove terribly damaging. For example, I could not bear the thought of defending its provisions before Soviet dissidents whose human right to emigrate would in the future be denied them, because government officials found some "personal or professional reasons" to disqualify them (one of the new phrases introduced at Bern).

I *could* defend this document, I had told Washington, if they judged that we should say yes; but I did not *want* to defend it. Washington saw clearly the perils in the document.

Moreover, the Bern proposals would now form the *minimal* starting place for the achievement of a better document in Vienna—a better document that the United States could with honor and integrity accept. At the very least, we had strengthened the hand of U.S. negotiators in the future.

The reader can make an independent judgment. In the appendix, the final compromise at Bern is reprinted, side by side with equivalent passages from Helsinki and Madrid. The reader can see clearly that the modest forward steps made at Bern were more than matched by backward steps.

The decision in Bern was difficult. I was certain that it was the correct one. The subsequent movement by the Soviets in the direction of *glasnost* seems to show quite clearly that the direction we had pointed to in Bern was neither mistaken nor in vain.

Sometimes, in fact, in later Soviet announcements about *glasnost*, which began to break out during the late summer of 1986, I thought I heard many of my own arguments in Bern coming back to me from Moscow. My speech of May 1, "Toward an Open Soviet Union," had been given in the cold dark days surrounding fresh terrorist attacks on U.S. and Western European citizens, in the fear and the official silence surrounding the drifting fallout from Chernobyl and in the pronounced lack of movement concerning divided spouses, emigration, and the hardships of Jewish and Christian dissidents. Then, two months after Bern entered history, so did a fresh wave of *glasnost*. I greeted it with joy.

Still, *glasnost* must be judged by the same standards as were applied in Bern: deeds, not words. It must lead to long-term, regular compliance with natural human duties and with agreements freely entered into. It must result in institutional checks and balances, to protect against another retreat into abusiveness.

May the 278 million citizens of the Soviet Union—all its "ordinary people"—be awakened by the cry of *glasnost* and come to live as others live, in intellectual honesty and basic liberty. That is still the Helsinki dream, and mine.

33
Accomplishments at Bern

MR. CHAIRMAN: First, allow me to express my deep appreciation to the Helsinki Commission for the truly welcome support it provided to the U.S. delegation at Bern. From Michael Hathaway, your excellent executive director, to Deborah Burns and Barbara Edwards, who did outstanding administrative work under difficult conditions and often worked very late hours, and including all the tremendous research and liaison work performed by Sam Wise, Orest Deychakiwsky, John Finerty, and Robert Hand, the staff of this commission provided indispensable service to our delegation. I thank the commission—and each of them—profoundly.

I was especially grateful that Congressmen Hoyer, Ackerman, and Bustamante and other members of the delegation were able to be with us during the last seventy-two hours of the meeting. Their advice and counsel and the tact and reserve they exercised in dealing with the entire delegation are deeply appreciated.

Mr. Chairman, when I last reported to this commission (on March 18), I said that our goals in Bern would be "practical results." On March 18 I defined our first three goals in these exact words:

> We define "practical results" precisely. We mean movement in specific individual cases. And we mean an improvement in the general conditions for cross-border human contacts by individuals and associations. In addition, a successful meeting entails a careful review of the record of how CSCE commitments have so far been implemented.

Only in fourth place did I mention that our delegation would make a good-faith effort to achieve a strong final document, if a strong one was achievable. I spoke of the realism of the allies, neutral and nonaligned, in advance of the meeting and reported to you as follows:

> We do not, for instance, put a premium on producing a new document. Good language on human contacts already exists

Testimony of Michael Novak before the Commission on Security and Cooperation in Europe, June 18, 1986.

in the Helsinki and Madrid documents. We do not suffer from a shortage of texts. What the world suffers from is inadequate implementation of already existing texts.

It seems important to reread this testimony of mine on March 18, because it outlines quite clearly what our intentions were when we began. The subsequent record shows that we more than fulfilled these intentions.

Consider the first of our goals, movement on concrete cases. Back in mid-March it seemed—not only to me but to others on our delegation and to some staff members of this commission—that we would be lucky to see the Soviet Union resolve even as many cases as had been resolved on the occasion of the summit talks between President Reagan and General Secretary Gorbachev in Geneva last November; namely, thirty-three cases, of which twenty-five had been fully acted upon by mid-March.

Actually, in Bern there were some practical results. On May 20 the Soviet delegation informed us that their government was resolving two new cases and that resolutions could shortly be expected in many more. On May 26, the last scheduled day of the Bern meeting, the Soviet authorities in Moscow gave us the names of thirty-six families whose cases were to be resolved. They told U.S. embassy officials that another list of names would soon be forthcoming, and indeed within ten days we were given the names of an additional twenty-nine families. About 200 persons in all will be affected by these decisions when they come to fruition.

In this fashion the USSR did use the Bern meeting as an occasion for taking action on concrete cases. It is deeply regrettable that action was not taken on these cases in the normal process of fulfilling Helsinki commitments. It is regrettable that such decisions are made only upon political occasions. Nonetheless, our delegation made the argument, in Moscow and in Bern, that the road to confidence building lies through the treatment regimes extend to their own citizens and that we are working for the day when the USSR and its allies will deal with their own citizens according to the internationally recognized standards they themselves have signed. In this context, I choose to interpret Soviet movement on cases as a helpful movement. The more of this the better—until all Soviet citizens share in the free exercise of those rights recognized in the international agreements their government has freely signed.

Further, the Romanian delegation resolved about half the list of twenty-seven specific cases presented to it in the course of the Bern meeting. Outside of Bern, between April 11 and June 1, Romania approved for emigration nearly 1,200 people from our representation list. These actions clearly reflected the current state of U.S.-Romanian relations with respect to Romania's most-favored-nation status. The Bulgarians resolved twelve of eighteen U.S. representation list cases the week before the Bern meeting opened.

Second, Mr. Chairman, we aimed at movement in "general conditions." Here our review of compliance showed that there *had* been positive movement in several Eastern European countries. The borders of several are much more open today than in 1975. There are many areas, however, in which the situation of human contacts, in the USSR, Bulgaria, and Romania in particular, has deteriorated. Administrative practices were shown to be in many respects worse than they had been in 1975.

The delegation from the USSR was driven to say on several occasions that, under the new general secretary, there would be a new "spirit," new "practices," and a reform of legislation and administrative procedures in the area of human contacts. This was in the nature of a promise, not in the nature of evidence cited. Before granting credence, it is proper to insist on evidence. Still, the delegation from the USSR did at least promise reform, in accordance with the promises General Secretary Gorbachev made to President Reagan in Geneva and at the Twenty-eighth Party Congress. Until evidence is forthcoming, skepticism is in order. Nonetheless, the invitation has now been issued to hold the USSR to fresh promises.

Our third goal was an intensive review of compliance. Such a review did go on for nearly five weeks, since the NATO nations had agreed to use their time in presenting new proposals to explain from the past record why such proposals are now needed. On one day, for example, sixteen of nineteen speeches presented evidence of abusive, noncompliant practices in the USSR, East Germany, Bulgaria, and other Eastern nations. This drumbeat—often low-key, factual, and nonpolemical—continued day after day. Many veterans of the CSCE process said that the Bern review of compliance was the most thorough, objective, and calm of any in the history of the CSCE.

In part, this was because the main points about compliance had already been established at Madrid, Ottawa, and Budapest. Thus the Soviet delegation in Bern only tentatively argued that the effort by an assembly of nations to monitor compliance in the field of human contacts represented "interference in the internal affairs" of the USSR. That line was dropped almost instantly. Instead, the Soviet delegation and some others chose, when criticized, to attack the critic. They did so typically with wild, loose, and passion-inflamed rhetoric, careless of accuracy and evidence, usually based upon criticisms of the West made by westerners, and on the whole rather more damaging to the attacker than to the attacked. In responding to specific charges, we chose to welcome even such attacks, poor as they were, as a way of urging the USSR and its allies to open themselves further to the legitimacy of mutual criticism from abroad, as well as to internal criticism. Open criticism is the way scientific inquiry proceeds. Open criticism is also the way political reform advances.

As in Ottawa and in Budapest, we realized from the beginning in Bern that achieving an acceptable final document would not be likely. But halfway through the conference, and after Chernobyl, it became obvious that the USSR and its allies might wish to achieve a final document in Bern. The question remained whether this would be substantive progress or propagandistic progress. We had promised to make a good-faith effort to work for a strong final document if a strong document were achievable. From the beginning we had ruled out a weak one.

At 4 A.M. on Monday morning, May 26, the day the conference was scheduled to end, the Soviets broke off all-night negotiations. As at Ottawa and Budapest, at that point we had no document. Until then the Eastern bloc had refused to agree to the original Western proposals even in their modest strength and had instead introduced damaging loopholes and qualifications. They were not willing to go very far. All that had been left on the table was a pale imitation of the strong proposals the Western nations had agreed to and tabled as BME 47.

Of course, it could be argued that some of the compromise proposals offered "marginal" or "modest" steps forward. But some of them also took steps *backward* from Helsinki. This typically happened in one of three ways: (1) in some cases, the compromise language was weaker than Helsinki; (2) in some cases, new loopholes were introduced into the Helsinki process; (3) in some cases, the point of view of the compromise proposals subtly slipped away from the general obligations already agreed to under Helsinki and began to treat those obligations, given existing violations, as goals we need to make progress toward. This last point deserves comment. Helsinki represents obligations agreed to by participating states; it does not represent goals to be striven for. To treat Helsinki obligations as goals toward which progress must be made is to alter the character of the Helsinki Accords in a potentially fatal way. They are not goals but general obligations.

Mr. Chairman, three or four of the compromise proposals may at first glance appear to represent the largest among the "modest" steps forward. Among these, for example, are the proposals on postal and telephonic communication and on religion. Under close analysis the compromise resolution on postal and telephone service has one good quality and one weakness. The good point is that it would bring documented abuses in this area under the compliance review of the Helsinki process. The weakness is that the proposal basically reminds the participating states of obligations that they already bear under existing international conventions, which are nonetheless being flagrantly abused.

As for the proposal on religion, the compromise formulation is not only far weaker than the modest original Western proposal. It is in virtually the same form that the Western nations had rejected during the negotiating process. The West had rejected this form for three reasons: (1) no less than other citizens, religious citizens have universally recognized rights to travel and to receive publications through the mail; (2) the restriction of the proposal to official "representatives" of religious organizations—but *not* to "individual believers"—is an intolerable infringement of universal rights; and (3) the right to receive and to carry with them religious publications and religious objects is confined to the extremely narrow limit of "for their own use"—that is, not even for the use of their congregations or fellow believers. This is an intolerably narrow reading of basic human rights.

Mr. Chairman, I said in Bern that the compromise document did make *some* marginal advances. But when one looks at the sum total, one must add up the minuses as well as the pluses. No one asserted that the pluses are more than "modest"; some said "marginal." But when you count in the minuses, even these modest gains are reduced. Moreover, the judgment one must make is whether the demonstrated record of noncompliance on large and basic issues, amply documented during our debates, truly gives hope that even "modest" or "marginal" improvements in new language will be taken seriously, when already existing large obligations are not. Judgment must be focused on the probabilities of future compliance.

First, then, it is essential to compare the last-minute compromise proposals with the corresponding texts of Helsinki and Madrid. One must do this critically, with an eye hardened by experiences of violations since then. Second, one must compare them as well with the original Western proposals on the same subjects. What are the pluses and the minuses? How does the whole add up? Our judgment was and is that the negatives either outweigh, or come close to outweighing, the positives.

Next, one must factor in the demonstrated record of noncompliance on matters large and small. In that context our judgment is that the negatives clearly outweighed the positives. To accept the

165

Bern compromise would have been to accept a document that could accurately be characterized in this way: some of its proposals merely repeat Helsinki provisions already being violated; some of its provisions are weaker or more flawed than Helsinki; some (such as the one on religion) would have established possibly damaging precedents; and a few, at best, went modestly beyond Helsinki. (Even these last, alas, sometimes advance more *specific* language but in a way that detracts from general obligations that already cover such specifics.)

In terms of policy, the most important point in the Helsinki process is its credibility. Solid words must not be allowed to become empty words. Agreements entered into merely to have agreements cannot be allowed to diminish public trust. Above all, agreements cannot be allowed to weaken the trust of those who suffer today because of large-scale and systematic noncompliance. In such circumstances, to enter into certain kinds of agreements would be a fraud.

Mr. Chairman, I told this commission last March 18 that the goals of my delegation would be (1) movement on concrete cases, (2) efforts to bring about greater compliance in specific types of cases, and (3) a thorough review of violations of the Helsinki Accords. I leave it to this commission to judge how well we achieved the three goals we set out to achieve.

I also told this commission that our delegation would not accept a weak document. I said then that the integrity of the Helsinki process depends first of all upon credible compliance, rather than on the addition of more words. I again leave it to this commission to judge whether, in difficult circumstances, we kept our word and showed proper judgment on the specific document at hand.

Finally, Mr. Chairman, I am more convinced than when I undertook this assignment that the CSCE process is worth every ounce of energy that this nation can put into it. That process depends on taking words with utmost seriousness, words signed by heads of government of thirty-five participating states. The CSCE process has borne great fruits in some countries in Eastern Europe and has heightened standards of international behavior. More than that, a newcomer to the CSCE process notices immediately the extent to which the language of Western ideals permeates not only the Helsinki Accords and the Madrid Concluding Document but also the daily debates in plenary discussions and working groups. Even the Marxist countries rarely speak a Marxist language; even they are often obliged to use the language (though not following the practice) of open societies. In the context of human rights, the importance of words is very great.

Mr. Chairman, looking forward to Vienna, when the whole range of the Helsinki Accords will be under discussion, the allies have a much better opportunity to make real progress in the areas of human rights and human contacts—for three reasons. First, the range of subjects on the table will be larger, greatly expanding the scope for meaningful negotiations. Second, the process will be open ended; to achieve meaningful progress, it will allow a period much longer than six weeks. Third, in Ottawa, Budapest, and Bern, the allies have taken great pains to arrive at common, strong proposals. These proposals, carefully hammered out, already at hand, form a magnificent platform for real progress under the "third basket." In addition, a thorough and documented review of noncompliance is now part of the full record from which Vienna can proceed.

Mr. Chairman, the work of the Helsinki process is extremely important for millions of human beings. The work of this commission in furthering that process is vital. Permit me once again to thank this commission for the support it gave my delegation, before, during, and now after the Bern meeting.

34
Breakthrough in Bern*

Michael Novak, American ambassador to the Bern Conference on Human Contacts, brought considerable credit to the U.S. at that gathering last month by refusing to sign yet another agreement for the Soviets to violate. Critics who charged that he jeopardized the Helsinki "accord" couldn't be more wrong.

The final hours of the six-week-long conference went something like this. At 10 P.M. May 25, the U.S. told its allies that the proposals tentatively agreed to were not strong enough to get Washington's approval. Negotiations went on through the night. At 4 A.M. the Soviets walked out, dooming the regular negotiations. Around 9 A.M. the neutrals and nonaligned tabled a compromise. After consulting with Washington, Mr. Novak rejected the package at about 2 P.M. Later, the West German foreign minister, Hans-Dietrich Genscher, called U.S. Secretary of State Shultz from Ankara to pressure the U.S. to reconsider. The *Times* of London said, "U.S. goes out on a limb in spoiling consensus at East-West meeting."

Before we talk about "spoiling" a conference we ought to have some notion what it was supposed to do. The six-week-long Bern meeting was designed to review the record of the 35 signatory states regarding the human-contacts provisions of the third "basket" of the 1975 Helsinki Accords. These provisions concern the reunification of spouses and families, freedom of travel, cultural exchanges and the like.

The U.S. position, as Ambassador Novak put it, was that what is needed is "not more documents but more compliance." Translated into policy, this means that the U.S. will not put its name to any more agreements unless those agreements are a clear, full step forward. That was the reason for signing at Madrid; that was the reason for refusal in Bern. Whatever its application, the rationale is eminently sound. As Anatoly Shcharansky reminded us recently, weak agreements only make those suffering behind the Iron Curtain more despondent. They are taking the tough line on the front; the least

*Editorial, *Wall Street Journal*, June 4, 1986.

Western diplomats can do is to remember them in between the caviar and cocktail parties.

On the surface some of the language in the compromise document doesn't look so bad. It has sections about allowing people to travel and go on family visits, but then introduced new language such as "when personal and professional circumstances permit." It's not hard to see that the insertion of such conditions as "when personal and professional circumstances permit"—innocuous in the West—can mean all the difference in the world in such countries as the U.S.S.R. that control those circumstances. After all, the reason we have politicians trotting halfway around the globe to argue over negotiating tables whether this wife should be permitted to see that husband is that those on the Eastern part of the divide make them political issues.

When you take in the total picture you begin to see that Mr. Novak's refusal to sign amid mounting pressure was a courageous decision made in the best interests of the people for whom the conference was called. Together with the Reagan administration's decision last week on SALT II and Mr. Reagan's own refusal in Geneva to be pressured into another meaningless agreement, it points to a new resolve in American policy: The U.S. will no longer agree to anything just for the sake of agreement. This will strengthen the hand of the negotiators the next time round, e.g., the general review of Helsinki scheduled for November in Vienna. Most important, it signals that the Americans are serious enough about negotiation to reject language that doesn't represent progress.

35

Taking Helsinki Seriously*

Is the Helsinki process worth it? There are many who say no. I have seen clear evidence to the contrary, in the Bern meeting just concluded.

The Helsinki Final Act is nearing its eleventh anniversary this August. It set in motion a novel institution—the Conference on Security and Cooperation in Europe (CSCE)—an institution with no headquarters, no staff, no permanent budget: rather a "process," a series of meetings on topics crucial to Europe and North America, from security questions to economics to human rights and human contacts. Its most recent meeting was in Bern, Switzerland (April 15–May 27), on the "human contacts" provisions of Helsinki (family reunification, family visits across borders, tourism, professional travel, and the like). My assignment was to head the U.S. delegation, meeting with thirty-four others from Europe and North America.

During the six weeks in Bern, the Western and neutral nations painstakingly reviewed the deterioration of compliance with the Helsinki Accords—including serious declines in emigration for family reunification and in family visits and the enforced isolation of Soviet citizens from contact with foreign visitors. Noncompliance in other hard-line states (such as Bulgaria's horrible assault upon its Turkish minority) was also demonstrated in detail. One has not often seen the USSR and some of its allies so totally on the defensive, day after day. They were obliged to defend their record in the light of Western values, for these are the values enshrined in the Helsinki Final Act and the 1983 Madrid Concluding Document.

Here an important element came to light: several of the Marxist nations have far better records than the USSR. The borders of Yugoslavia (a nonaligned country) and Hungary, for example, are, if not quite open, remarkably so; emigrants and visitors leave in great numbers. Poland, too, except for arbitrary restrictions on certain persons, allows great latitude for travel in and out. Thus the *reasons* for noncompliance in certain Marxist nations cannot be said to be simply "ideological," required by the nature of a Marxist social sys-

Wall Street Journal (European edition), June 4, 1986.

tem. The reason for noncompliance seems to have to do with the fear and insecurities of a particular ruling class, among them that of the USSR, of Bulgaria, and of Czechoslovakia.

This increasing differentiation among Eastern states is one of the best fruits of the Helsinki process. Some peoples and cultures do seem to be far more classically European in their tendencies and inclinations, less Asiatic, less closed, less fearful. In this differentiation lies considerable hope for further evolution in the future.

Indeed, one of the most remarkable realities of the Helsinki process is the gradual emergence of a single European language about individual rights, openness, liberality, and freedom—a new set of moral standards governing the behavior of states. Even in defending themselves, the Soviet delegation often employed liberal values, as in mentioning with pride the number of persons who went abroad for family reasons in 1985 (120,000)—about as many go through Heathrow airport in a single day, one Western delegate dryly observed.

On human rights and human contacts, to repeat, the Helsinki standards of judgment have unmistakable Western roots. The Soviet defense against such principles is to introduce loopholes. Only so can they continue to allow reasons of state to prevail over individual liberties.

In this respect, the Bern meeting permitted a thorough factual review of the way Soviet administrators today frustrate actual compliance with the philosophical principles they committed themselves to in Helsinki and Madrid. They affirm shining principles up ahead, then invent labyrinthine bureaucratic obstacles that prevent individuals from ever reaching them.

With this in mind the United States decided, in the end, not to give consent to a last-ditch compromise document presented on a take-it-or-leave-it basis in the last hours at Bern. Here is how it happened. At 4 A.M. on May 26, the USSR delegation walked out on the regular negotiations, dooming any final document. At 9:30 A.M. the neutral and nonaligned nations presented a last-ditch compromise. Having made a good-faith effort to walk the last mile in seeking a strong, sound final document, the United States reluctantly found this compromise too weak, too modest, and too vulnerable to loopholes to give consent to, even though, in some cases grudgingly, other delegations were willing to go along with it.

It is very difficult to stand alone; to do so is not done lightly. Some Western colleagues deeply desired even modest progress. They have seen how modest steps in the past have led to tangible fruits for their citizens. Not all governments are as cynical as the USSR: there is slow but real progress elsewhere. This is a strong argument.

Nonetheless, the United States judged that any weakening of the fundamental principles of Helsinki and Madrid would bring the whole Helsinki process into a deepening crisis of credibility. In the last-minute compromise document, a large majority of the strong initial Western proposals were missing, dramatically weakened by compromise, or riddled with loopholes offering cynical governments new language by which to justify future noncompliance.

For example, Helsinki had already affirmed the commitment that governments will "favorably consider applications for travel" for family visits. The Bern compromise, in trying to resolve some specific obstacles to family travel, would also have introduced a new loophole: "when personal and professional circumstances permit." Cynical governments able to change personal and professional circumstances at will would be able to use such a new loophole massively.

Another proposal, permitting travel by persons irrespective of their cultural, ethnic, or national origin, would have been limited to travel to other "participating states"—thus excluding Israel. This whole paragraph had thus to be stricken from the compromise. Again, the proposal on travel for religious reasons was restricted to "representatives" of religious institutions, not including individual believers, and would have allowed the importation of religious publications and religious objects only "for their own use"—that is, not for distribution to their congregations.

Taken all together, the proposals contained in the compromise document were defended by some as, at most, "modest steps." Each had been compromised downward or subjected to dangerous loopholes. Cumulatively, however, they would later have been bitterly attacked by an increasingly skeptical public, for however unintentionally moving away from the clearer and more general commitemnts of Helsinki and Madrid. Given the record of noncompliance on clear and general commitments, the compromise document marked scant advance over previous documents and offered little promise of better compliance in the future. And it would have offered some fresh excuses for the noncompliant. That risk was too real to accept.

Thus the final legacy of Bern is that the words of Helsinki must be regarded with utmost seriousness—honored in substance, complied with in practice. Helsinki gave us, as it were, the Ten Commandments. The emphasis now should be on better compliance. Intellectual rigor is the best guarantor of the integrity and credibility of the Helsinki process. That means making reality match commitments, and guarding existing commitments jealously.

36
Epilogue

Alexander Ginzburg, the first of the Soviet dissidents and the founder of the first samizdat (unofficial, underground) publication, attended a discussion of glasnost at the American Enterprise Institute on July 29, 1987, to introduce the new magazine 'Glasnost,' an English translation from the new Soviet magazine by that name that had recently begun appearing in Moscow. Ginzburg had suffered for two years in a Soviet labor camp, being released in 1979 in an exchange for Soviet spies (a cruel practice in itself, such an exchange). After the discussion, I moved to the back of the room to shake his hand and to express my admiration. Instead, he told me of a telephone message he had received the night before from Moscow, from a colleague who told him to thank me for "the brilliant refusal" to sign the Bern document. Ginzburg told me that this action "had saved the Helsinki process."

These words made all the agony of confronting the negative reaction in Bern disappear. I had known then it was the correct judgment. I would not have wanted to live with the thought that I myself had signed a bad document. I dreaded the thought that some of its phrases would later be used by Soviet officials to justify rejection of the claims of dissidents, refuseniks, and others to basic rights. But on the day of the decision I could not know for sure whether those most at risk would agree with me. I could not be certain whether our no might lead to greater closure than before. Our clear aim was to convince Gorbachev that the United States was serious about compliance. In the event, later that summer, the Soviets began to take the large steps toward openness that we had urged them to. It is quite a joy to see so many persons whose names were mentioned in Bern in freer circumstances than before. May glasnost continue, spread, and grow. For it, too, the test is deeds, not words.

Appendix

The columns in the appendix table beginning on the next page place three sets of texts side by side. Such an analysis was requested by Senator Alfonse D'Amato at the hearings of the Helsinki Commission. Column one offers the authoritative texts from the Helsinki Final Act, the Madrid Concluding Document, or both. Column two offers the full-strength proposals originally tabled by the West in Bern. Column three provides the compromise text at Bern, rejected by the United States for falling short of the texts of Helsinki and Madrid. Column four offers brief comments on the Bern compromise, drawn from an analysis by the Human Rights Bureau of the U.S. Department of State. Further explanation is offered in my testimony before the Helsinki Commission, chapter 33 in this book.

COMPARISON OF HELSINKI/MADRID LANGUAGE
WITH BERN's FINAL COMPROMISE PROPOSALS
AND ANALYTICAL COMMENTS

Helsinki/Madrid	Western Proposals (as tabled)[a]	Final Compromise Proposals	Analytical Comments
[H] In order to promote further development of contacts on the basis of family ties the participating states will favourably consider applications for travel with the purpose of allowing persons to enter or leave their territory temporarily, and on a regular basis if desired, in order to visit members of their families. [M] The participating states will favourably deal with applications relating to contacts and regular meetings on the basis of	1. Timely attention should also be given to travel for visits in cases of important family matters such as births, marriages, religious or civil ceremonies and other important family occasions; travel for important public and religious holidays; travel to visit the grave of a family member.	1. When dealing with applications for family visits to take due account of important family events and their significance for the applicant.	Existing language covers all family visits. Specific mention of "important family events" could imply that the general commitment is not absolute. "Take due account" is weaker than the general commitment in Helsinki and Madrid to "favourably consider" and "favourably deal" with family visit applications.

family ties, reunification of families and marriages between citizens of different states and will decide upon them in the same spirit.		
[H] [As above] [M] [As above]	2. To deal favorably with applications from members of a family to travel together for the purpose of contacts and regular meetings on the basis of family ties, when personal and professional circumstances permit.	Ability of a family to travel together implicit in existing language. Making this explicit would have been a small addition, but "when personal or professional circumstances permit" is a critical new loophole that cynical governments would undoubtedly use to justify refusals.
6. In fulfillment of their commitments to facilitate freer movements and contacts, remove, *inter alia*, obstacles to the ability of members of a family, who so desire, to travel together for the purpose of contacts and regular meetings on the basis of family ties.		
[H] Applications for temporary visits to meet members of their families will be dealt with without distinction as to the country of origin or destination: existing re-	[From the Swiss-Austrian Proposal (BME 36), Part I] The participating states agree to recommend to their governments: to extend the range of persons entitled to family visits, 3. To deal favorably with applications for family contacts without distinction as to the age of the applicant, when personal and professional circumstances permit.	Similar to 2; "without distinction as to the age of the applicant" would have made explicit the fact that existing documents make no such distinctions, but the same crippling

177

Helsinki/Madrid	Western Proposals (as tabled)[a]	Final Compromise Proposals	Analytical Comments
quirements for travel documents and visas will be applied in this spirit.	including visits to and from more distant relatives; to deal favorably also with applications by members of the active working population without distinction as to the age of the applicant as well as applications by more than one family member for joint family visits; to increase the number and frequency of family visits; to expand the range of recognized purposes for family visits, taking due account of important family events and religious occasions such as births, marriages, educational or academic		loophole would have given states a new excuse for refusals.

	events, religious and civil holidays and celebrations, anniversaries and others.	4. To facilitate travel for the purpose of family reunification, consider in a humanitarian spirit and give importance to consideration of the wishes of the parties desiring to be reunited.	"Give importance to consideration" is a weak formulation. The East made clear that "consider in a humanitarian spirit" in this context would permit the invocation of ties to remote family members, and possibly to society at large, to deny reunification in the family's preferred destination.
[H] The participating states will deal in a positive and humanitarian spirit with the applications of persons who wish to be reunited with members of their family. . . . They will deal with applications in this field as expeditiously as possible. [H] Applications for temporary visits to meet members of their families will be dealt with without distinction as to the country of origin or destination: existing requirements for travel documents and visas will be applied in this spirit. [M] The participating states will favorably deal	7. Give primary importance to the wishes of the parties desiring to be reunited, in particular their wishes in regard to the country of settlement, in facilitating the exit of persons for the purpose of family reunification.		

Helsinki/Madrid	Western Proposals (as tabled)ᵃ	Final Compromise Proposals	Analytical Comments
with applications relating to . . . reunification of families.			
[H] The participating states will deal in a positive and humanitarian spirit with the applications of persons who wish to be reunited with members of their family. . . . They will deal with applications in this field as expeditiously as possible.	3. In implementing their commitments with regard to family reunification, give special attention to requests for exit documents and facilities submitted in order to reunite minor children with their parents.	5. To give special attention on humanitarian grounds to cases of reunification of families where minor children are involved.	Implicit in existing language. "On humanitarian grounds" contains same risk of abuse as in 4. Singling out a new category of minor children for "special attention" could imply lessening of attention to cases, no matter how urgent, if they do not involve such children.
[H] Applications for the purpose of family reunification which are not granted may be renewed at the appropriate level and will be reconsidered at reasonably short intervals by the authorities of	[Swiss-Austrian Proposal, Part II] The participating states agree to recommend to their governments . . . to simplify and reduce the number of administrative requirements for family	6. To provide that any document necessary for an application procedure be easily accessible to the applicant, also in cases of renewed application, and to prolong the validity of such documents so that	Accessibility of documents and prolongation of their validity add to existing language. "Unless a change of essential significance for the consideration of the application occurs in the

the country of residence or destination, whichever is concerned; under such circumstances fees will be charged only when applications are granted. [M] The participating states will provide the necessary information on the procedures to be followed by the applicants in these cases and on the regulations to be observed, as well as, upon the applicant's request, provide the relevant forms.	visits such as special authorizations, permits, or attestations; to simplify and accelerate procedures for applying for, processing of and deciding on family visits; not to limit unduly the validity of visas for family visits; in cases of renewed application to take into consideration documents already supplied by the applicant in connection with a previous application; to reduce the minimum exchange requirements for family visits.	circumstances of the applicant" is a new loophole that leaves the state considerable arbitrary discretion. they remain valid throughout the application procedure, unless a change of essential significance for the consideration of the application occurs in the circumstances of the applicant.
[H] The preparation and issue of such documents and visas will be effected within reasonable time limits. [H] The participating	[As above]	7. To simplify practices and gradually reduce administrative requirements for family visits and to accelerate procedures for applying for, processing Vague commitment to simplify practices and gradually reduce administrative requirements is new but not likely to have practical significance;

Helsinki/Madrid	Western Proposals (as tabled)[a]	Final Compromise Proposals	Analytical Comments
states intend . . . gradually to simplify and to administer flexibly the procedures for exit and entry.		of and deciding on family visits.	commitment "to accelerate procedures" is reformulation of existing commitment to deal with applications "expeditiously" and "within gradually decreasing time limits."
[H] The preparation and issue of such documents and visas will be effected within reasonable time limits. [M] [The participating states] will decide upon these applications in emergency cases for family meetings as expeditiously as possible, for family reunification and for marriage between citizens of different states	[Swiss-Austrian Proposal, Parts I and II] The participating states agree to recommend to their governments: to extend the range of persons entitled to family visits, including visits to and from more distant relatives; to increase the number and frequency of family visits; to expand the range of recognized purposes for family visits, taking due	8. To do their utmost to deal with applications for family visits favorably and in time, taking into account the purpose of the visit, and not to limit unduly the validity of the visas involved.	To deal with applications "in time" would have been a marginal addition to existing language. But the ambiguous qualifier, "taking into account the purpose of the visit," would provide a pretext for denials. "To do their utmost" and "unduly" are weak.

account of important family events and religious occasions such as births, marriages, educational or academic events, religious and civil holidays and celebrations, anniversaries and others; not to limit unduly the validity of visas for family visits.

in normal practice within six months and for other family meetings within gradually decreasing time limits.

---

2. In order to simplify the application procedures for family reunification, prolong the validity of the application forms and other related documents so that these documents remain valid throughout the application procedure; provide that any document necessary for an application procedure be easily accessible to the applicant, also in case of renewed application.

[H] Applications for the purpose of family reunification which are not granted may be renewed at the appropriate level and will be reconsidered at reasonably short intervals by the authorities of the country of residence or destination, whichever is concerned; under such circumstances fees will be charged only when applications are granted. [M] In case of refusal ap-

---

9. In cases of renewed application for family contacts to take into consideration documents already supplied by the applicant in connection with a previous application, unless a change of essential significance for the consideration of the application occurs in the circumstances of the applicant.

Consideration of documents supplied with a previous application adds to existing language but is qualified by same damaging loophole as in 6.

Helsinki/Madrid	Western Proposals (as tabled)[a]	Final Compromise Proposals	Analytical Comments
plicants will also be informed of their right to renew applications after reasonably short intervals.			
[H] The participating states will deal in a positive and humanitarian spirit with the applications of persons who wish to be reunited with members of their family, with special attention being given to requests of an urgent character—such as requests submitted by persons who are ill or old. [M] [The participating states] will decide upon these applications in emergency cases for family meetings as expeditiously as possible.	1. [The participating states] in implementing their commitment to deal favorably with and to decide upon, as expeditiously as possible, applications for travel relating to family matters, [will] pay immediate attention to those of an urgent humanitarian character, including *inter alia* travel to visit a seriously ill or dying family member; travel of the aged and those with urgent medical needs; on the basis of a medical cer-	10. In implementing the provisions of the Madrid Concluding Document to deal favorably with and to decide upon, as expeditiously as possible, applications for travel relating to family matters, pay immediate attention to those of an urgent humanitarian character, including *inter alia* travel to a seriously ill or dying family member, travel of the aged and those with urgent medical needs on the basis of a medical certificate which should not	Largely a restatement of existing language, adds travel of the aged and those with urgent medical needs to previous examples of persons entitled to expedited treatment.

be delayed, by a medical authority in the country of residence, travel to attend the funeral of a family member.

11. In emergency cases to intensify efforts by all the authorities concerned in order to decide upon applications in such cases as expeditiously as possible, using to the fullest possible extent existing modern means of communication so as to ensure the most rapid and effective cooperation among them, ensuring that the charges for priority treatment in emergency cases do not unduly exceed standard charges.

Restatement of existing language, without precise detail of the original Swiss-Austrian proposal.

tificate which should not be delayed, by a medical authority in the country of residence; travel or visit the grave of a family member.

[Swiss-Austrian Proposal, Part III] The participating states agree to recommend to their governments . . . in emergency cases to intensify efforts by their respective local, regional and central authorities in order to decide upon applications for urgent family visits as expeditiously as possible and within, at most, three days; to use to the fullest possible extent modern means of communication so as to ensure the most rapid and effective cooperation both at a national and an international level;

[H] [In addition to the above] [The participating states] will lower where necessary the fees charged in connection with these applications to ensure that they are at a moderate level. . . . Fees will be charged only when applications are granted.
[M] [The participating states] will decide upon these applications in emergency cases for family meetings as expeditiously as possible.
[M] [The participating states] will, where necessary gradually reduce fees

Helsinki/Madrid	Western Proposals (as tabled)[a]	Final Compromise Proposals	Analytical Comments
charged in connection with these applications, including those for visas and passports, in order to bring them to a moderate level in relation to the average monthly income in the respective participating state.	to ensure that fees charged for priority treatment in emergency cases do not unduly exceed standard fees.		
[H] The receiving participating state will take appropriate care with regard to employment for persons from other participating states who take up permanent residence in that state in connexion with family reunification with its citizens and see that they are afforded opportunities equal to those enjoyed by its own cit-	[An Eastern bloc proposal]	12. To ensure, where necessary through bilateral arrangements, that persons who have settled permanently on their territory for the purposes of family reunification or marriages between citizens of different states, enjoy economic and social opportunities equal to those enjoyed by their own citizens, in con-	Restatement of Helsinki, with qualified reference to "bilateral arrangements."

izens for education, medical assistance and social security.

[H] [The participating states] confirm that religious faiths, institutions and organizations, practising within the constitutional framework of the participating states, and their representatives can, in the field of their activities, have contacts and meetings among themselves and exchange information.

[M] The participating states reaffirm their commitment fully to implement the provisions regarding diplomatic and other official missions and consular posts of other participating States con-

formity with the laws and regulations of the participating states in question.

[An Eastern bloc proposal]

13. To consider favorably in accordance with the laws and regulations of the country of residence applications by migrant workers legally resident on their territory for contacts and regular meetings on the basis of family ties, reunification of families and marriages between citizens of different states and to reaffirm the right of such workers to free access to diplomatic and other official missions and consular posts, as well as their right to maintain contacts with their country of origin.

Yugoslav proposal. Implicit in existing language.

Helsinki/Madrid	Western Proposals (as tabled)[a]	Final Compromise Proposals	Analytical Comments
tained in relevant multilateral or bilateral conventions, and to facilitate the normal functioning of these missions. Access by visitors to these missions will be assured with due regard to the necessary requirements of security of these missions.			
[M] [The participating states] confirm that the presentation or renewal of applications in these cases will not modify the rights and obligations of the applicants or of members of their families concerning inter alia employment, housing, residence status, family support, access to social, economic or educa-	[Swiss-Austrian Proposal, Part IV] The participating states agree to recommend to their governments . . . to make renewed efforts to give full effect to the provision of the Madrid Concluding Document, that the presentation or renewal of applications in these cases will not modify the rights	14. To give full effect to the provision of the Madrid Concluding Document, that the presentation or renewal of applications for family meetings, family reunification and marriage between citizens of different states will not modify the rights and obligations of the applicants	Restatement of existing language.

188

tional benefits, as well as any other rights and obligations flowing from the laws and regulations of the respective participating state.
[H] [The participating states] confirm that the presentation of an application concerning family reunification will not modify the rights and obligations of the applicant or of members of his family.

[H] [The participating states] confirm the right of the individual to know and act upon his rights and duties in this field.
[M] The participating states will provide the necessary information on the procedures to be followed by the applicants in these cases and on the

or of members of their families concerning *inter alia* employment, housing, residence status, family support, access to social, economic and educational benefits, as well as any other rights and obligations flowing from the laws and regulations of the participating states in question.

and obligations of the applicants or members of their families concerning *inter alia* employment, housing, residence status, family support, access to social, economic or educational benefits, as well as any other rights and obligations flowing from the laws and regulations of the respective participating state.

13. In order to ensure that the inhabitants of their countries are made widely aware of the fundamentals of their national legislation concerning travel abroad, publish within one year all laws, regulations and procedures—including criteria for refusal—gov-

The compromise text is derived from the Western proposal. While the commitment "to publish" was retained, the time limit was omitted and specific reasons for travel were added. An initially constructive proposal thus became little more than a restatement of Madrid

15. In order to ensure that the inhabitants of their countries are made widely aware of the fundamentals of their national legislation concerning travel between states to publish and make easily accessible, where this has not already been done, all laws and

Helsinki/Madrid	Western Proposals (as tabled)[a]	Final Compromise Proposals	Analytical Comments
regulations to be observed, as well as, upon the applicant's request, provide the relevant forms.	erning decisions to permit their citizens to leave their country, on a permanent or temporary basis; and take steps to help make the laws that are in force accessible to all strata of the population of the country.	administrative regulations relating to travel for family, personal or professional reasons, on a permanent or temporary basis.	language.
[H] The participating states . . . intend . . . gradually to simplify and to administer flexibly the procedures for exit and entry; to ease regulations concerning movement of citizens from the other participating states in their territory, with due regard to security requirements.	17. Abolish, for their nationals, the requirement to obtain an exit visa in order to leave their country; issue exit visas to foreigners residing on their territory as expeditiously as possible and without any conditions other than those that may arise as a result of legal proceedings still in process.	16. To issue exit visas, where required, for foreigners residing on their territory as expeditiously as possible, subject to the conditions specified in national legislation.	This compromise text is also derived from a Western proposal, which was a commitment by the participating states "to abolish, for their nationals, the requirement to obtain an exit visa in order to leave their country; and issue exit visas to foreigners residing on their territory as expeditiously as possible." The

		compromise text retained only the expeditious issuance of exit visas to foreigners, a slight addition to existing language which is nullified by a damaging loophole—"subject to the conditions specified by national legislation."
[M] The participating states reaffirm their commitment fully to implement the provisions regarding diplomatic and other official missions and consular posts of other participating states contained in relevant multilateral or bilateral conventions, and to facilitate the normal functioning of those missions. Access by visitors to these missions will be assured with due regard	17. In order to ensure better conditions for consular, legal, and medical assistance for citizens of participating states traveling in other participating states, to consider, if necessary, adhering to the Vienna Consular Convention and concluding, if needed, complementary bilateral agreements.	Restatement of existing language, with new reference to Vienna Consular Convention. Access to missions has often been impeded in Eastern countries.
[An Eastern bloc proposal]		

191

Helsinki/Madrid	Western Proposals (as tabled)[a]	Final Compromise Proposals	Analytical Comments
to the necessary requirements of these missions. [M] The participating states will endeavour, where appropriate, to improve the conditions relating to legal, consular and medical assistance for citizens of other participating states temporarily on their territory for personal or professional reasons, taking due account of relevant multilateral or bilateral conventions or agreements. [M] The participating states will endeavour, where appropriate, to improve the conditions relating to legal, consular		Consider adhering to relevant multilateral instruments in the field of legal assistance such as civil and family matters, and concluding, if necessary, bilateral agreements on such questions. Consider favorably the solution, *inter alia* by concluding bilateral agreements, of problems that may arise in connection	

with medical assistance, especially in cases of sudden illness or injury resulting from accidents.	18. To facilitate the creation of satisfactory conditions, where they do not yet exist, for receiving tourists as well as persons who are participating in contacts and exchanges in fields such as culture, science, religion, education and sport and their representatives or corresponding institutions and organizations meeting among young people, and sport.	Restatement of existing language, with coverage extended to tourists and persons in the field of religion.
	[An Eastern bloc proposal]	
and medical assistance for citizens of other participating states temporarily on their territory for personal or professional reasons, taking due account of relevant multilateral or bilateral conventions or agreements.	[M] [The participating states] also reaffirm their willingness to take, within their competence, reasonable steps, including necessary security measures, when appropriate to ensure satisfactory conditions for activities within the framework of mutual cooperation on their territory, such as sporting and cultural events in which citizens of other participating states take part.	

Helsinki/Madrid	Western Proposals (as tabled)[a]	Final Compromise Proposals	Analytical Comments
[H] The participating states intend to further the development of contacts and exchanges among young people by encouraging: increased exchanges and contacts on a short or long term basis among young people working, training or undergoing education through bilateral or multilateral agreements or regular programmes in all cases where it is possible; study by their youth organizations of the question of possible agreements relating to frameworks of multilateral youth cooperation . . . the development, where possible, of exchanges,	[An Eastern bloc proposal]	19. To favor the conclusion, between youth and student organizations, of bilateral and multilateral agreements or programs designed to develop contacts among young people and to promote exchanges among them.	Restatement of existing language.

		Same as 19. Possibly useful reference to need of agreement for replacement of an invitee could be used to legitimate practice of such replacement to suit the interests of official organizations. Also, a dim shadow of the original Western proposal,
	20. To favor visits and exchanges between universities and other higher educational institutions of different participating states, including direct contacts among their students and teachers, taking into account in that context that	
contacts and cooperation on a bilateral or multilateral basis between their organizations which represent wide circles of young people working, training or undergoing education. [M] The participating states will encourage contacts and exchanges among young people and foster the broadening of cooperation among their youth organizations. [H] The participating states . . . express to these ends their intention in particular . . . to expand and improve . . . cooperation and links in the fields of education and science, in particular by . . . promoting the conclusion of direct arrangements be-	4. In implementing their commitments under the Final Act and the Madrid Concluding Document further to develop contacts among nongovernmental organizations and associations, and to facilitate wider travel by their citizens for	

Helsinki/Madrid	Western Proposals (as tabled)[a]	Final Compromise Proposals	Analytical Comments
tween universities and other institutions of higher education and research, in the framework of agreements between governments where appropriate. [M] The participating states will contribute to the further improvement of exchanges of students, teachers and scholars and their access to each other's educational, cultural and scientific institutions.	personal or professional reasons, remove existing impediments which prevent individuals and the institutions and organizations which they have freely established and joined from maintaining contact, communication and organizational ties with similar organizations in other participating states without need of official sponsorship or approval; permit individuals invited by such groups to travel to other participating states so that they are not replaced by another individual without the consent of the inviting organization.	an invited person may be replaced when the inviting party agrees.	whose emphasis on "nongovernmental institutions" was rejected by the Eastern bloc.

[H] In order to expand existing links and cooperation in the field of sport the participating states will encourage contacts and exchanges of this kind, including sports meetings and competitions of all sorts, on the basis of the established rules, regulations, and practice.

20. Mindful of their willingness expressed in the Final Act to encourage contacts and exchanges in the field of sport, including sports meetings and competitions of all sorts, for the purpose of promoting this aim, encourage direct sporting exchanges between them at local and regional levels, as well as at national and international levels, and take steps to remove existing obstacles to such exchanges.

21. To encourage direct sporting exchanges between teams and participants at local, regional and international levels on the basis of mutual agreements, to encourage exchanges and contacts among young people and their organizations, both governmental and nongovernmental, as well as the holding in this connection of bilateral and multilateral cultural, educational and other activities and events by and for young people, in the spirit of the recommendations contained in the documents adopted by the United Nations in the framework of the international youth year, concerning broadening contacts and exchanges

Implicit in existing language. "On the basis of mutual agreements" is a new qualification. Reference to international youth year is harmless but not useful.

Helsinki/Madrid	Western Proposals (as tabled)[a]	Final Compromise Proposals	Analytical Comments
[H] The participating states . . . make it their aim to facilitate freer movement and contacts, individually and collectively, whether privately or officially, among persons, institutions and organizations of the participating states, and to contribute to the solution of the humanitarian problems that arise in that connection.	10. Recalling their belief, as expressed in the Final Act and the Madrid Concluding Document, that the development of contacts is an important element in the strengthening of peace and understanding among peoples, remove legal and other obstacles restricting or inhibiting contacts on their own territory between their citizens and resident or visiting citizens of other states.	among young people from different states. 22. To develop the possibilities of contacts on their territory between their citizens and citizens of other participating states in accordance with the relevant provisions of the Helsinki Final Act and the Madrid Concluding Document.	The original Western proposal, from which this text is derived, was to "remove legal and other obstacles restricting or inhibiting contacts on their own territory between their citizens and resident or visiting citizens of other states." The compromise formulation obscures the real problem of laws and regulations that restrict such contact. It adds nothing of practical value to existing language.
[No previous language]	14. Recognizing that the freedom to establish and maintain communication is essential for effective	23. To guarantee, in accordance with the Universal Postal Convention and the	Ensuring the rapid delivery of mail is new to the CSCE process, restating binding commitments un-

	human contacts, guarantee the freedom of transit of postal communications in accordance with the Universal Postal Convention, thus ensuring the rapid and unhindered delivery of personal mail; ensure all the conditions necessary to carry on rapid and uninterrupted telephone calls in accordance with the International Telecommunication Convention; respect the privacy and integrity of all such communications.	International Telecommunications Convention, the freedom of transit of postal communications. To ensure the rapid delivery of correspondence, including personal mail, and to ensure the conditions necessary for rapid telephone calls, including the use and development wherever it is possible, and to respect the privacy of all such communications.	dertaken elsewhere. Ensuring conditions for rapid telephone calls and for "privacy of all such communications" are additions to existing language. "Wherever it is possible" is a wide loophole to the provision on direct dialing systems.
[No previous language]	15. [The participating states] should carefully review all outstanding applications for travel for the purpose of family reunification and for other purposes related to the	24. To review carefully all applications for travel for the purposes of family reunification and for other purposes related to the aims of the part of the Helsinki Final Act and	The review of applications is a marginal addition to existing language, but, given noncompliance with previous commitments to decide "favorably" and "expeditiously," this new

Helsinki/Madrid	Western Proposals (as tabled)[a]	Final Compromise Proposals	Analytical Comments
	aims of the part of the Helsinki Final Act and the Madrid Concluding Document dealing with human contacts with a view to ensuring that these applications are being dealt with in a manner consistent with the relevant provisions of those Documents. They further recommend that such reviews should be repeated at regular intervals.	Madrid Concluding Document dealing with human contacts, which have not yet been decided upon or to which a formal answer has not yet been given, with a view to ensuring that all applications are dealt with in a manner consistent with the relevant provisions of those documents.	formulation is unlikely to be of any practical value.
[M] [The participating states] agree to give favorable consideration to the use of bilateral roundtable meetings, held on a voluntary basis, between delegations composed by each participating state to	19. Give favorable consideration to the practice of periodically holding bilateral meetings and round tables between delegations, whose composition is to be determined by each participating state, to	25. To give favorable consideration to the practice of holding—on the basis of mutual agreement—bilateral meetings and round tables between delegations, whose composition is to be de-	Reformulation of existing possibility to hold bilateral round-tables on all human rights issues.

discuss issues of human rights and fundamental freedoms with an agreed agenda in accordance with a spirit of mutual respect with a view to achieving greater understanding and cooperation based on the provisions of the Final Act.

deal with questions concerning the promotion of contacts among their citizens, institutions and non-governmental organizations. The aim of these meetings and round tables will be to improve and develop co-operation in the humanitarian field among the participating states, to implement more fully the relevant provisions set forth in the Final Act and in the Madrid Concluding Document, and to bring about as promptly as possible a satisfactory solution to outstanding humanitarian cases. In particular, on the occasion of such meetings and round tables, the participating delegations should also proceed to a mutual exchange of ex-

termined by each participating state, to deal with questions concerning the development of contacts among persons, institutions and organizations. One of the aims of these meetings and round tables will be to contribute to improving and developing cooperation in the humanitarian field among the participating states, including the discussion of current humanitarian issues.

Helsinki/Madrid	Western Proposals (as tabled)[a]	Final Compromise Proposals	Analytical Comments
	haustive information and full details, and to their updating in the event of changes, on the laws, procedures and practices in force in the respective countries with regard to applications for travel abroad submitted by citizens with a view to contacts and regular meetings on the basis of family ties, reunification of families and marriages between citizens of different states.		
[H] The participating states . . . declare their readiness to these ends to take measures which they consider appropriate and to conclude agreements or	[The Eastern bloc proposal]	26. To consider widening the practice of inter-governmental agreements, protocols or programs concerning exchanges in various fields,	Harmless but not useful.

arrangements among themselves, as may be needed. [H] [The participating states] confirm that religious faiths, institutions and organizations, practising within the constitutional framework of the participating states, and their representatives can, in the field of their activities, have contacts and meetings among themselves and exchange information. [M] The participating states reaffirm that they will recognize, respect and furthermore agree to	concluded on multilateral or bilateral basis, in contributing to the carrying out and development of contacts among persons, institutions and organizations of the participating states. 18. In fulfillment of their commitment under the Madrid Concluding Document to implement further the relevant provisions of the Final Act so that religious faiths, institutions, organizations and their members can develop contacts and meetings among themselves and exchange information, promote the possibilities for individual believers and communities of believers to establish and maintain	Restatement of existing language. New references to pilgrimages, postal communications, and religious publications and objects. "For their own use" is a damaging qualification—i.e., persons could not bring or receive sufficient copies for a whole congregation, synagogue, or parish. Important reference in original Western proposal to "individual believers" deleted. 27. In implementing the relevant provisions of the Final Act and the Madrid Concluding Document, to promote the possibilities of religious faiths, institutions, organizations and their representatives to establish and maintain personal contacts and communication with religious faiths, institutions and organizations and their representatives also in other countries, including travel, pilgrimages, and postal communica-

Helsinki/Madrid	Western Proposals (as tabled)[a]	Final Compromise Proposals	Analytical Comments
take the action necessary to ensure the freedom of the individual to profess and practise, alone or in community with others, religion or belief acting in accordance with the dictates of his own conscience. [M] [The participating states] will further implement the relevant provisions of the Final Act, so that religious faiths, institutions, organizations and their representatives can, in the field of their activity, develop contacts and meetings among themselves and exchange information.	personal contacts and communication with fellow-believers and communities of believers also in other countries, including travel, pilgrimages, assemblies and postal communications; respect the ability of believers and communities and believers to acquire, receive and carry with them religious publications and related materials.	tions and to allow them, within the field of their activity, to acquire, receive and carry with them religious publications and religious objects for their own use.	

[No previous language]

5. Reaffirming the role that individuals and organizations have to play in contributing to the achievement of the aims of the CSCE process as well as the commitment of the participating states to develop further contacts among governmental institutions and nongovernmental organizations and associations, encourage the setting-up and facilitate the unimpeded implementation of town-twinning arrangements between authorities most directly concerned in order to develop direct contacts between their citizens.

28. To encourage the setting-up and to facilitate implementation of town-twinning arrangements between institutions, organizations and citizens of their respective countries.

The introduction of "town-twinning," a bilateral practice, is new to CSCE but not of any practical significance.

NOTE: The compromise proposal entirely omitted Western proposals on national minorities (joined by the Yugoslavs), on the circumstances of exits, on dual nationals, on trade unions, and on the right of nationals to passports. These original full texts follow:

8. Mindful of the legitimate desire of persons belonging to national minorities and regional cultures on their territories to have contacts with persons in other states with whom they have close affinities, refrain from placing obstacles in the way of members of such minorities and regional cultures seeking to maintain contacts of this kind, including contacts through travel and communications.

9. In dealing favourably with an application for travel for the purposes of family contact or family reunification with an individual family member who has permanently left his country of origin, ensure that the application will not be prejudiced by the circumstances in which this family member left his country of origin.

11. In implementing their commitments, as expressed in the Final Act and the Madrid Concluding Document, to facilitate freer movement and contacts among persons, give special attention to and deal favourably with applications from their citizens or nationals who are also recognized as citizens or nationals by another state to visit that state or to settle there.

12. In implementing their commitment under the Final Act and the Madrid Concluding Document further to develop contacts among nongovernmental organizations and associations, and to encourage, as appropriate, direct contacts and communications between trade unions and their representatives, remove existing impediments which prevent freely established trade unions, their members and their representatives from maintaining contact, communications and organizational ties with similar organizations in other participating states without need of official sponsorship or approval.

16. Recognize the right of their nationals to be issued with a passport, or with any other document allowing travel abroad, without delay and without any other conditions than those specifically laid down by the law in conformity with international commitments. Reasons should be given for any refusal to issue a passport or travel document and means of appeal should be available.

a. At the appropriate places, I have also supplied relevant portions of the (very long) Swiss-Austrian proposal on family visits (BME 36, as tabled), where portions of it figured in the final compromise.

This book was edited by Dana Lane
and Trudy Kaplan of the
Publications Staff of the American Enterprise Institute.
The text was set in Palatino, a typeface designed by Hermann Zapf.
Coghill Book Typesetting Company, of Richmond, Virginia,
set the type, and Edwards Brothers Incorporated,
of Ann Arbor, Michigan, printed and bound the book,
using permanent acid-free paper.